LOVE

Each Other

Other Books by Martin Down

Speak To These Bones
Streams Of Living Water
Building A New Church Alongside The Old
Deluded By Darwinism?
The New Jerusalem
Low Cost - High Price (with Theresa Cumbers)

LOVE

Each Other

By

MARTIN DOWN

emblembooks

www.emblembooks.co.uk

This first edition published in Great Britain 2012

ISBN 978-0-9559594-6-2

Cover design by Adam Jackson.

Published by Emblem Books, Swaffham, UK
www.emblembooks.co.uk

How good and pleasant it is when
brothers live together in unity.
Psalm 133.1

Contents

Chapter One

A NEW COMMUNITY

Jesus said, ‘This is my command: love each other,’ (John 15.17). Just before this, he had said, ‘You are my friends,’ (15.14). John himself repeats Jesus’ words, ‘Dear friends, let us love one another,’ (1 John 4.7).

In one sense, as Jesus said, this is not a new commandment. The Ten Commandments could always be summarised in the two great commandments: ‘Love the Lord your God with all your heart and with all your soul and with all your mind; and love your neighbour as yourself’ (Matthew 22.37-39). Love has always been at the heart of the life that God our Creator has willed for us, because God is love (1 John 4.16b). And yet Jesus does give his disciples a new commandment: ‘Love each other.’

This is not the same thing as loving our neighbours as ourselves: that applies to all our relationships and to all our neighbours. The new commandment that Jesus gives us is to love each other within the fellowship of the church, and it is not to love our fellow believers as we love ourselves, but to love them as Jesus loves us: 'Love each other as I have loved you,' (John 15.12).

We are so familiar with these words that we rarely stop to ask ourselves, 'How do we do it?' It is as if this most challenging of all commandments does not need thinking about. What are the implications for our life together as Christians? What does it look like in practice, to love one another? Why do we so often stumble over it and fail in it? What can we do to love one another more or better?

This commandment is so fundamental to the Gospel that it is strange that there are so few books written about it or sermons preached about it. There are books galore about the Bible, doctrine, worship, prayer, healing, prophecy, ethics, leadership, or social justice, but not many about loving one another. Christian fellowship means more than a nod or a handshake as we leave church on a Sunday morning. There seems to be a gap where teaching, as distinct from exhortation, about loving one another ought to be.

Loving each other is the thing that people in the world find hardest, even impossible to do. History is largely a tale of wars. The daily news is largely a catalogue of crime and mayhem. Family life, especially as portrayed in the television soap operas, is only too often a story of quarrels and estrangements. What passes for popular entertainment seems largely to mean dramas about people shooting each other, hitting each other, and shouting at each another.

These are all things from which we need to be saved: not only from the guilt and power of our own personal sins and shortcomings, but from this chronic inability to love each other and to live together in harmony.

Loving one another is first of all about being together in community, and secondly about staying together without this constant feuding and fighting. It is difficult, even impossible, in the world. It is also difficult in the church, as history has shown. But for the followers of Jesus it is not meant to be impossible. Jesus never requires us to do the impossible. In the church, we are supposed to be able to love one another. We have the resources of grace and power that are needed to be successful in this most difficult of all enterprises: loving one another. We need to study how to do it.

Loving each other ought to be a major preoccupation for Christians in every generation. It is essential to the Gospel. It is at the very heart of the call of Jesus, for time and for eternity. But it must be a subject of particular importance and relevance in the generation in which we live.

We live today in societies that are increasingly fragmented, in which more and more people are feeling isolated and lonely. These are amongst the consequences of the way we live now. The progress of technology, affecting every aspect of our lives, has brought many blessings and improvements, lightening the burden of toil and facilitating every form of communication. But it has also brought new problems in its wake, not the least of which is the disintegration of older forms of community and the increasing isolation of individuals.

These modern problems present the church with both a special opportunity and a special responsibility. The opportunity is to communicate the Gospel through friendship in an increasingly friendless world. The responsibility is to offer people the example and experience of a new community of friends, one that transcends the natural communities that are breaking down, and one that fulfils the longing of every human heart to be loved and to belong.

It all depends on the quality of our life together in the local church: do we really love one another? Are we really friends?

Chapter Two

THE LONELY SOCIETY

No mourners. No minister required.

'Dear God,' I thought, 'what sort of a tragedy is that?'

I was waiting in the vestry at the crematorium, before the funeral that I was about to conduct, and I was reading the crematorium's running order for the day. It was the instructions for the cremation that had preceded mine that caught my eye: "No mourners. No minister required.'

What sad story lay behind that bleak message, and how many other people come to their final end with neither family, nor friends, nor neighbours, to mourn their passing or to say goodbye? Had this man been some old tramp, a vagrant, who had simply perished with cold, sleeping out in a shop doorway or under a hedge, and been picked up by the police and put in a coffin? Is that what happens to the homeless in the end?

Or was this an old woman who had spent the last years of her life sitting in a silent circle with other people that she did not know in some residential home, until she finally expired, without relations or friends? Or, worse still, was this the funeral of some young person who had run away from home and died of a drug overdose in some squalid squat, where nobody knew or cared who he was?

Loneliness is an increasing phenomenon in our urbanized, industrialised, globalized societies. A Report in 2010 by the UK Mental Health Foundation found that 60% of young adults between the ages of 18 and 34 said that they felt lonely often or sometimes. A similar Report by Adrian Franklin and Bruce Tranter of the Housing and Community Research Unit of the University of Tasmania also found that 'loneliness has reached unprecedented levels' in Australian society.

Increasing loneliness is the consequence of complex changes in the way that we live, none of which were designed to increase loneliness, but many of which have produced this as an unintended by-product. In the old rural community of the village, or even in the streets of old terraced housing, no-one was unknown. Only a few, mostly elderly, people lived on their own; the majority were only too closely crammed together in large families and small houses, with tentacles reaching into many other households in the village or the surrounding streets.

These old communities were not paradise on earth, but in them everybody belonged. Even the ancient, slightly batty, recluse who lived with her cats and swore at her neighbours, was known, and knew herself to be known; she might live a solitary life but she was an insider not an outsider in the community.

But the world has changed. Historically, the railway, the bicycle, the bus, the car, and now the aeroplane, have taken families and friends away all over the country and all over the globe. Even when I was a child, growing up in a London suburb during the Second World War, my grandparents on both sides lived within walking distance of our home, and my sister and I were both born in my grandmother's house.

My own grandchildren, on the other hand, were born in hospitals in the United States of America and in France, and while two of them have subsequently returned with their parents from the USA, they still live 150 miles away across the middle of England, and the other three are permanently domiciled with their parents in Burgundy. It is not that we do not love each other, simply that the globalisation of work and travel have moved us a long way away from one another. We live apart, not together.

For many people, removed in this way from blood relations, the place of family in their lives has been taken by friends. It is significant that the cult American sit-com of the nineties was simply called *Friends.*

This series followed the lives of six twenty-somethings, living together in a New York apartment block. The authors, David Kane and Marta Kaufman sold the series to NBC in 1994 as, ‘about friendship, because when you're single and in the city, your friends are your family.’

But such friendships are invariably fluid. People move jobs, move flats, move in and out of sexual relationships, develop new interests or pastimes, make new friends and drift away from old ones, usually much more frequently than the six characters in *Friends,* who survived together in the virtual world of television for ten years. Long friendships are rare, and lifelong friendships rarer still, all made harder to sustain, like family relationships, by the increase of mobility.

A survey of nearly 1,500 adults in the United States recently revealed that a quarter had *no-one* to whom they could talk about important matters in their lives, and another quarter had only *one* such friend. This may seem astonishing in itself, although the results are similar to other surveys conducted in other places. But it is even more astonishing when compared with a similar survey carried out in the US twenty years before. In those twenty years the number of people with no close friends had doubled, and the average number of close friends that people reported having, had declined from three to two.

It is in the same twenty years that mobile phones and internet social networking have exploded. Are these technological substitutes for face-to-face relationships the cause or the effect of the increasing loneliness in our societies, or both? Either way, it amounts to the same thing: a text on a mobile phone is not the same thing as a hug and a kiss, and an internet pal is not likely to pick up the kids for you after school.

Virtual friendship is virtual: it is not friendship. Sarah Brennan of the UK charity *YoungMinds* says, 'The young people we work with tell us that talking to hundreds of people on social networks is not like having a real relationship and when they are using these sites they are often alone in their bedrooms.'

Despite our fantasies about friends taking the place of families, we are no more adept at keeping up with our friends in today's world than we are at keeping up with our families. When all is said and done blood is thicker than water, and if our family ties have been loosened by mobility, how much more the ties of friendship. The first that I know of the death of an old friend may be the non-arrival of the yearly Christmas card.

Another cult television programme since 1985 has been the Australian soap-opera *Neighbours.* But just as *Friends* portrayed a fantasy world of friendship, so *Neighbours* portrays what for most people is a fantasy world of neighbourliness, an 'if-only' world that they might like to inhabit, but that is as far away from their own neighbourhood as Australia is from England.

My wife and I live on a new housing estate on the outskirts of a market town. There are fourteen households that would count as our immediate neighbours. We want to be neighbourly, and at one time or another we have invited all our neighbours into our house. After five years, of these fourteen we exchange occasional greetings in the street with some ten of these neighbours, with two we have failed to make any contact at all, and with only two or three do we have any more than a nodding acquaintance.

For the most part we all come and go in our motor cars with at most a wave to each other; we have different interests and occupations, and our paths hardly cross. If people are in any sort of trouble, they are more likely to visit the doctor, call the police, or deal with the social services, than call on or confide in their neighbours. Experiences will vary, but I guess that our experience is more typical of 21st century urban and suburban life than *Neighbours.* Nothing, neither friends nor neighbours, have taken the place of family or the older communities in modern life.

Other changes, moral rather than physical or technological, have also had the effect of increasing the incidence of loneliness. The generations that have grown up in the last sixty years have thrown off the shackles of a morality that disapproved of divorce, illegitimate children, and sex before marriage.

These changes in our social *mores* are directly linked to the decline of Christian belief and practice in Western society. When people stopped going to church, it did not occur to them that much of the fabric of society would collapse around them as a result, but that is what has happened.

Marriage, the lifelong union of one man and one woman, is an integral part of Biblical revelation: take away trust in that revelation, and the institution of marriage totters as well. Quickie divorces, one night stands, legalised abortions, could all be made to sound like new freedoms, and were indeed made to sound like that in the 1960s, but, as well as all manner of other undesirable social consequences, this sexual revolution has ended up for many people in a new isolation.

In 1901, 512 divorces were granted by the law courts in Great Britain. A new Act of Parliament in 1937 opened the door a little wider, and in 1961 27,000 divorces were granted. But the biggest change in the law in Britain occurred in

1969 with the passing of the Divorce Reform Act. By 1971 the annual divorce figures had climbed to 80,000, by 1981 to 157,000, and they have hovered around 150,000 divorces *per annum* ever since.

Recent slight falls in this number are due only to the fact that fewer people are marrying in the first place, another social trend that we shall examine in a minute. These statistics mean that nearly half of all marriages in the UK can be expected to end in divorce. A similar trend can be traced in all Western countries over the last 100 years.

Of course, these legal statistics do not reveal the full story. Before 1969 many more families broke up and many more marriages ended in separation than the divorce courts recorded, and many of the couples that did stay together did so in a state of more or less disharmony and strife. In the debates about the liberalisation of the divorce laws it was often stated that many people who preserved the outward forms of matrimony were in fact living a lie, and there was no doubt some truth in that. Nevertheless the possibility and the practice of quick, easy and cheap divorce has meant that many more marriages and families are breaking up, leaving one or more of their members living alone.

Divorce can seem the obvious way out of a stressful and unhappy period in a relationship, or a satisfying way of taking revenge for a marital betrayal, but few people stop to count the cost in the longer term. The majority of those who divorce remarry sooner or later, and some of these second or even third marriages are more successful than the first, but there are many other divorced people who do not find another partner and face the prospect of growing old by themselves.

This is perhaps particularly the case for women. When wives are divorced they usually get custody of the children, and the job of looking after and bringing up the kids occupies most of their time and energy in their early years on their own. During this time, it is difficult for a woman to reinvent a social life outside the home, and men may be less inclined to take on a ready-made family with a new partner.

The crunch comes for the woman when the children fly the nest and acquire lives, jobs, careers, relationships and families of their own. By this time mum has lost her youthful sex-appeal and has less prospect of finding someone else to share her later years. A woman, who was interviewed during the debate over the reform of the divorce laws in Ireland, said, 'A woman voting for divorce is like a turkey voting for Christmas.'

Alongside the increased incidence of divorce there has come in the last forty years a sudden collapse in the incidence of marriage itself. In 1971 there were nearly 500,000 marriages in the United Kingdom; by 2007 this was down to under 300,000. More startling still, in 1971 first marriages were nearly 400,000, while in 2007 under 200,000. In less than forty years, at a time when the population has steadily increased, the number of first marriages has more than halved.

Most people of all ages hold on to the dream of finding a lifelong partner to love and care for them, but increasing numbers of young people are unwilling to commit themselves to this dream or to accept the limitations on their freedom that this would imply. Australian researchers Franklin and Tranter concluded: 'The paradox of contemporary loneliness is that our unswerving pursuit of individual freedom means we are, at the same time, unwilling to commit to the enduring and stable bonds we crave as lonely people.'

There is no longer any social disapproval of sex before marriage, indeed such disapproval has been replaced by a presumption that such sexual activity is normal and healthy, even a human right. Many such relationships remain casual and short-term, whilst others drift into cohabitation. But cohabitation is not equivalent to marriage. Not only are cohabiting couples more likely to split up than married people, but married couples who have cohabited before marriage are more likely to split up than married couples who have lived separately.

The biggest single factor in determining the permanence of a relationship is the level of commitment that both parties bring to it. The difference between marriage and cohabitation is the difference in the level of commitment that the partners invest in the relationship. Marriage is the public proclamation of this commitment to one another: 'for better, for worse, for richer, for poorer, in sickness and in health, to love and to cherish till death do us part.' This public proclamation, before family and friends, before the representative of the State and perhaps before

God himself, strengthens and confirms that commitment. It is an acceptance of responsibility for one another, and for the children that may result from the relationship, that is lacking in other, more temporary sharing arrangements.

Franklin and Tranter again: 'The fact that marriage seems to insulate people so well against loneliness demonstrates how it may be the *nature* of the bond rather than relationships per se (their number and their frequency of interaction) that are important to understand in studies of contemporary loneliness.'

The result of the present regime of sexual freedom is that young people drift from onc relationship to another, throughout their twenties and often into their thirties, without the incentive to marry and settle down that the sexual urge provides. It can be made to sound like having fun, but it also involves stress and anxiety. A dating agency that surveyed 500 young, single people found that 51% reported stress from loneliness, against only 18% who reported stress from problems with money or debt. The problem with musical chairs is that when the music stops there is always someone for whom there is no chair, and it may be you.

The current boom in house-building in Britain is made necessary by two main factors: immigration and increased single occupancy. At present, single occupancy accounts for 30% of households, and the government expects this to rise to 38% by 2026. The fastest growth in the rate of single occupancy is amongst the 25-44 year-olds, with the fastest growth of all amongst 35-44 year-old never-married men. We are breeding a generation of loners.

Even such signs of moral progress as the emancipation of women and the Welfare State have had unforeseen adverse consequences in terms of our lives together. The economic emancipation of women in the last fifty years has removed the financial dependence that used to bind housewives into marriage: walking out on their husbands or showing their husbands the door was simply not a viable option when the whole family depended on the husband's income for their mutual support.

Today, the woman has as many opportunities for employment as the man of the house, and even if both partners are not already working and earning a separate income, neither partner now feels bound to continue in a marriage simply for financial reasons. If the efforts of a single mother to support herself and her children are not sufficient, the Welfare State is ever ready to come to her help with housing and other benefits. The economic disincentives to separation and divorce of former years have largely disappeared, opening the door to freedom for some and to temptation for others.

All this adds up to a society in which adults of all ages are more and more likely to find themselves living alone and suffering from loneliness. Most people are financially independent from at least their twenties onwards so that the need to live together and support onc another in families is not there.

The moral climate and the focus of society have shifted away from an emphasis on duties and responsibilities and towards an emphasis on rights and self-fulfilment. This again makes it harder for us to maintain faithful, long-term relationships with the give-and-take that such relationships always involve. One way and another we are less good than previous generations at trading off present satisfactions for the sake of future rewards; we have less patience with life and with each other.

Loneliness or living alone can be a problem at any time in our lives, but it seems to afflict us most at both ends of adult life, the young but especially the old. Of the baby-boomer generation, now entering retirement, one third are now experiencing loneliness or living alone. Swinging may have seemed great in the Sixties; it does not seem quite so great in your own sixties or seventies or eighties.

This was the first generation of free-lovers and divorcees; but now many of them, even up to half the women, find themselves no longer in work, their children grown up, divorced or widowed, their friends dying, and their expectation of this sort of life continuing longer and longer.

The seemingly infinite expansion of the market in residential and nursing homes reflects both the increase of longevity and the increase of people living without anyone else, whether family or friends or neighbours, to love and support them at home.

And that is how some of us end up on the funeral list as, '*No mourners, no minister required.*'

Chapter Three

'IT IS NOT GOOD FOR THE MAN TO LIVE ALONE'

It was never meant to be like this.

'It is not good for the man to live alone.' It is God himself who said it (Genesis 2.18), the One who can be presumed to know more about us than we know about ourselves. Up to this point in the creation story at least, most people would probably agree that this is true.

At this point God has made only the man, Adam, and God's first observation on the subject of his new creature is that it is not good for the man to be alone. If he had made the woman first, he would have said the same thing about her: 'it is not good for the woman to be alone'. It is an observation about humanity in general, not exclusively about the male half of it. It is an observation about our need, not just for practical help with the business of living, though that is important, but about our need for companionship and love.

So what does God do? First, he brings to the man the beasts and the birds, and the man names them (Genesis 2.19-20). Whatever people are inclined to make of these creation stories, especially the one that follows about the creation of woman, there is an uncanny accuracy about these observations of human nature. If someone discovers a new species of insect in the Amazon rain-forest or a new species of fish on the floor of the deep ocean, the first thing that they do is give it a name.

It seems to be our mission on Earth to name things, with all that implies. Moreover, the birds and the beasts provide us with some sort of company. Domesticated animals and birds provide many lonely people with the only companionship that they have. To come home to a dog, a cat, or even a budgerigar is, for many people, better than coming home to an empty house. People talk to their pets and even swear that their pets 'talk' to them, and perhaps the budgerigar does. It is at least something else in the house that is alive and responds to its human owner. But an animal or a bird is not really what a man, or a woman, wants and needs.

So in the story, God creates another human being to help Adam and to keep him company (Genesis 2.21-25), a woman. For Jesus and his followers, as for the Jews, this story provides the basis for our understanding of God's original will and purpose, both to meet our need for companionship and to be the means of reproduction (Genesis 1.28).

Our sexuality is God's design and gift: he made us male and female (Genesis 1.27). He did not need to do so. There are organisms and species that reproduce asexually. There are important biological advantages to sexual reproduction but it is not inevitable. God chose to make us male and female, not because it was the only way to reproduce, but because two are better than one: 'It is not good for the man to live alone.' 'For this reason a man will leave his father and mother and be joined to his wife and they shall become one flesh' (Genesis 2.24).

This one verse tells us all that we need to know about God's intention for us in our nature as sexual beings and beings in need of help and companionship. The formation of this relationship between a particular man and woman is what we call marriage. Marriage has three dimensions and, like the union of the man and the woman themselves, 'what God has joined together, let man not separate' (Matthew 19.6).

Marriage is for the reproduction of children, the companionship of husband and wife, and the satisfaction of their desire for one another which unites them physically and binds them together as one. This one verse, Genesis 2.24, answers all our questions, as it answered the questions of those who came to Jesus (e.g. Matthew 19.3-6), about the sins and shortcomings to which we are prone in our sexual relationships: sex outside, whether before or after marriage, divorce, homosexuality, and other sexual perversions such as paedophilia and bestiality - these are all, in different ways, perversions or divergences from the purposes of God.

It is important for us as Christians when addressing such issues that we emphasise not the sinfulness or unnaturalness of these human misdoings, but the loveliness and desirability of God's original plan. It is perhaps even more important that Christians live out God's original plan in their own lives, in their marriages and families, providing the world with winsome models and examples of this ideal in practice, even in a world in which, like everyone else, we fall short.

Marriage and the family are God's original remedy for loneliness and I believe that this pattern is still imprinted somewhere deep inside every human being. In spite of the contemporary prevalence of sexual promiscuity, cohabitation and divorce, I believe that every man and woman still longs for a stable, faithful, loving relationship that will last till the end.

This longing still crops up in the most surprising places. From pantomimes, which still end with the principle boy and girl coming down the steps in glittering white as they finally overcome all obstacles to marriage and happiness, to a popular song by David Bowie in 1977:

> Sometimes you get so lonely,
> Sometimes you get nowhere,
> I've drifted all over the world,
> I've left every place.
> Please be mine, share my life,
> Stay with me, be my wife.

Then, families grow: the family becomes the clan, the clan the tribe, the tribe the kingdom; people build cities and civilisations. The whole process is reflected in the stories of the Bible. God calls Abraham and his family, his clan, then the twelve tribes of Israel, then the nation and kingdom of David and Solomon.

Human society expands and takes on increasingly complex forms that require ever more elaborate degrees of organisation and administration. All this is foreseen within the providence of God: 'the authorities that exist have been established by God' (Romans 13.1). But as social groupings become larger and more complex, so they become more impersonal, and there is more danger that that longing and desire for personal companionship and love will be left unfulfilled.

In any society, marriage and the family remain the basic God-given way for these needs to be met, but where, for any reason, these institutions are weakened or undermined, people can be left struggling in a vacuum, deprived of supportive relationships.

Human beings have many needs. There are our basic physiological needs for our survival:

food and drink, sleep, and shelter from the elements, health and physical fitness. It is to provide for these needs, as much as for our more psychological needs, that we band together and form mutually trusting and supportive relationships, in marriage and the family, and in the wider society and economy.

None of us can provide for even these basic needs without the help of others. But we also have more complex needs that involve other people too: we need to feel accepted, valued, and esteemed by others; we need to be able to express our own gifts and personalities in creative and productive ways; we need to be able to give to others as well as receive from them; in short, we need to live our lives in community; we need to love and be loved.

This need for love begins at the same time as the need for our mother's milk, at birth, if not before. Dr Raj Persaad, in *The Mind: A User's Guide,* published under the auspices of the Royal College of Psychiatrists, says, 'Nurture and touch are basic human needs. Babies that are cuddled gain weight much faster than babies that are not touched. Traumatized children grow less well, and there is evidence that unhappiness and distress in childhood is linked to poorer heath in adulthood.'

Dr Spock, on whose advice in *Baby and Child Care* generations of children have been raised, says, 'There is only one real trick to raising a mentally healthy child: a loving, nurturing and mutually respectful relationship between you and your child.'

Love alone of course is not enough. As Richard Templar says in the *Rules of Parenting,* 'You have to give your children love. But there are a few other things you have to give them too: discipline, self-discipline, values, the ability to form good relationships, a healthy lifestyle, a range of interests, a decent education, a broad mind, the ability to think for themselves, an understanding of the value of money, the skills to be assertive, the ability to learn – and the occasional haircut.'

But the foundation of it all is love.

Our most important need of love, is the love of God. The first man, Adam, was made to have fellowship with God even before he was made to have fellowship with his fellow men and women. That is why the first and great commandment is this: 'Love the Lord your God with all your heart and with all your soul and with all your mind,' even before you love your neighbour as yourself, (Matthew 22.37).

Our relationship with God is more important than even our closest and most intimate human relationship. God alone is omnipresent: a presence from whom we cannot be separated by day or by night. Our relationship with God alone is eternal; from all our human lovers, friends and family, we shall be parted sooner or later by death, and only in the everlasting arms of God will we escape death ourselves. Our relationship to God survives eternally; our relationships with others may survive in him, but only in him.

However, to know the love of God for us, and to love God in return, as the source of all being and perfection - great and over-riding as this is - is not enough. If it were, then it would have been enough for the man to be alone with God as he was at the beginning. But God saw that the man needed human company and the love of other human beings for his completeness and happiness. And so, he created Eve, and she became the mother of all the living.

These human beings that God made were formed to be social creatures, made in the image of God, who is a sociable God, Father, Son and Holy Spirit. Man was made to live in companionship with God, in companionship with his wife and children, in companionship with other members of a wider society mutually providing for each other's needs, and in companionship with the animals and the whole creation. Paradise was a place of harmony, between God and Man, between man and woman, between man and man, between Man and Nature.

But the world as it is now is not the world as God made it or intended it to be. Sin, human pride and rebellion, the sinful human desire for independence from God and his commandments, have spoiled or ruined every aspect of God's creation. The temptations of the world, the flesh and the devil, and the very love of evil itself, have shattered all the harmonies that God at first created and intended: the harmony between God and Man, the harmony between man and woman, between parent and child, between brother and sister, between tribes and nations, between mankind and the animals, between the animals themselves, between mankind and the Earth, all have been broken and replaced by alienation and strife.

The dreadful mess that we see every day in the world around us, the wars and terrorism, the fears and suspicions, the oppression and violence, the family and social breakdown, the crime and vandalism, the lust and the greed, the waste and pollution, the neglect and abuse, the disease and death, and the loneliness, are all the result, directly or indirectly, of our wilful rejection of God and his ways.

God could easily have written his creation off as a failure. To look at the world today, its dismal past and its fearful future, is enough to make anyone despair of its redemption. But God did not despair or give up. He still loves the world that he made and everything in it. He sees the misery of his people and hears their cries, not just the cries of the people of Israel, but also the cries of every creature, the cry of every new-born baby and the cry of every wounded animal. Not a sparrow falls to the ground but God does not know it and feel for it.

And God has acted, and continues to act, for our salvation and for the redemption of the world that he has made. The Bible is the story of all that God has done to this end: of Plan B in God's gracious providence, his plan for the salvation and redemption of the world. It begins with the call of Abraham and culminates in the life, death and resurrection of Jesus. It will find its ultimate completion when Jesus comes again in power and glory.

In Jesus, God has done everything necessary for the redemption of the world. Jesus is the first-fruits of a new creation, a new creation that will eventually include the world and the universe itself. The invitation of Jesus to each one of us is to become part of this new creation, to be, as he says, 'born again' (John 3.3).

In the teaching of Jesus this new creation is called 'the kingdom of God'. The Kingdom of God is not a geographical reality, like the United Kingdom of Great Britain and Northern Ireland, or the Kingdom of Saudi Arabia. It is a spiritual reality: wherever God is loved, honoured and obeyed, there is the Kingdom of God. It is the 'place' where God rules and reigns.

In the present age we live in the overlap, between the old creation, in its spoiled and sinful state, and the new creation that is being renewed day by day until it comes to its final perfection.

We ourselves who believe in Jesus are being changed into his likeness from glory to glory, and prepared for a future of unimaginable joy: new heavens and a new earth, Paradise restored, the City of God. We need to try to grasp the breadth and length and height and depth of that hope, and an important part of it is the restoration of fellowship: the fellowship of the Kingdom.

The purpose of God in creation was not to create a man in isolation. It was to create men and women in community, in fellowship: in fellowship with God and in fellowship with one another. When people sin, their communion and fellowship is broken, both with God and with one another. Jesus came to redeem, not just individual men and women, but to fulfil the whole of God's creation purposes.

The completion of these purposes will see fellowship restored between God and Man: the dwelling of God will be with men, and they will be his people, and God himself will be with them and be their God. It will also see the restoration of fellowship between people and peoples: they shall beat their swords into ploughshares, and their spears into pruning hooks; nation shall not take up sword against nation, not will they train for war any more.

It even involves the restoration of fellowship and harmony within the natural world itself: the wolf will live with the lamb, the leopard will lie down with the goat, the calf and the lion and the yearling together, and a little child will lead them. Peace will reign over all the earth under the just and gentle sovereignty of the Prince of Peace.

The perfection or completion of all this will not be realised in this world, but in the New Jerusalem, in the world to come. But there are and there will be signs of all this even in this age, in the life of the church and in the lives of the followers of Jesus. In all its aspects there is a 'now' and a 'not yet' of the Kingdom of God, a 'now' and a 'not yet' that is revealed in the parables and teaching of Jesus, and in his mighty works.

The miracles of Jesus, miracles of healing and deliverance, miracles of multiplication of bread and stilling of storms, are all described as 'signs' of the Kingdom: they are a foretaste and a guarantee of the Kingdom that is both here at hand and still to come. In the same way the fellowship of the church is to be a sign of the

Kingdom: a foretaste, a pledge, of that eternal fellowship with God and with one another for which God made us and for which he is still preparing us.

Those of us who have witnessed the restoration of the healing ministry of Jesus in the church have rejoiced to see the sick healed and those in bondage set free. But we have to acknowledge that in our experience not all the sick are healed or all the captives set free.

Every healing and deliverance is a sign of the good purposes of God and a foretaste of the world to come, but we are not satisfied with what we see now, we long for more. Even so it is the same with the fellowship of the Kingdom: in the life of the church we experience some of the joy of fellowship with God and with one another, and yet there remain flaws and imperfections in our life together, and we long for something more.

We have seen how a recovery of the spiritual gifts and the power of the Holy Spirit have breathed new life into the church in the last one hundred years. We have seen how signs and wonders, and changed lives in the church, have convinced many that God is real, as they did in the ministry of Jesus. But I believe also that the more vividly a church, a body of Christians, can live out the fellowship of the Kingdom in their lives together, the more powerfully that church will attract others in this broken world, a world of broken families, broken societies, and broken lives.

Many, many people in our economically advanced, urban societies have a desperate need of belonging. One of the blessings that God wants to confer on those who turn to him is the blessing of love and fellowship, a love and fellowship that is liberating and life-giving. Therefore, at least one important focus in the life of the local church should be a focus on fellowship, the building up of the fellowship of the church, on preserving the unity that the Spirit gives, on being a sign of the fellowship of the Kingdom.

Robert Warren summarised the gospel for the 21st century in three sentences: 'God's way of being human has been revealed in Jesus. It is available to all through the Holy Spirit. It is now being demonstrated in a church near you.' One of the aspects of God's way of being human is to be human in the company of others. It is one of the tasks of the church to make that a reality in a place near to everyone, to demonstrate what it looks like in the world today, not in word but in deed.

This is no new message. It is the message that we have heard from the beginning: that we should love one another. The Apostle John who was writing this message went on immediately to draw the contrast with Cain who murdered his brother Abel. This message of love for one another is precisely the message that we need to hear in order to redeem that brokenness between man and man that began with the murder of Abel.

This is the only new commandment that Jesus gave to his disciples: that they should love one another. The good news is that it is possible for those who know the love of Jesus, and that at least a glimpse or foretaste of it is possible in the life of the local church.

Chapter Four

FELLOWSHIP IN THE EARLY CHURCH

From the beginning we see Jesus gathering around him a group of disciples. Some time before the formal nomination of the Twelve, we see Jesus building relationships with Andrew and Peter, Philip and Nathanael (John 1.35-51).

When the time does come for Jesus to choose his Twelve Apostles (Mark 3.13-19), it is clear that he is choosing them out of a wider circle of men who had begun to follow him. There are also women in this band. Three of them are named in Luke 8.1-3: Mary Magdalene, Joanna the wife of Chuza the steward of Herod, and Susanna.

By the time we come to the Day of Pentecost, we find that this group of disciples, both men and women, numbered about 120, including Mary the mother of Jesus and his brothers (Acts 1.14-15). When the Eleven decided that it was necessary to elect someone to take the place of Judas Iscariot in the number of the Twelve they apparently had no difficulty in selecting two men as candidates, men who had been with them the whole time, beginning from the baptism of John up to the day, recently, when Jesus had been taken up from them into heaven (Acts 1.21-22).

There was not always harmony within this group of followers. James and John caused some indignation amongst the others, when they or their mother came to Jesus and asked for special places for her sons (Mark 10.35-41). The Twelve were not a group of naturally like-minded men: Simon the Zealot would not have had a natural affinity with Matthew the tax collector.

The Zealots were fanatically anti-Roman and seethed, inwardly and sometimes outwardly, to see the Promised Land under the heel of a pagan power, whereas Matthew had made his living by collecting taxes for the very Romans that Simon hated. And even before Judas Iscariot turned betrayer, it would seem that he was under a certain suspicion as the keeper of the money-bag (John 12.6).

But this only emphasises how closely the Twelve, if not the wider band of followers, lived together: they had a common purse, filled presumably by the gifts of those whom Jesus had blessed, not least the rich women mentioned above (Luke 8.3). But this was a group that found its unity and cohesion, not in any natural or worldly identity of background or purpose, but only in their love and loyalty towards Jesus.

Jesus, then, during his ministry drew together a band of men and women who followed him, literally, from place to place, listened to his teaching, saw the miracles that he did, and shared a growing sense of comradeship and affinity with one another. When Mary Magdalene and the other women find the tomb of Jesus empty on the third day after his death, the first thing that they are told to do is to go and share the good news with Peter and the other disciples.

When we next meet these other disciples they are gathered together behind locked doors. In their grief and fear they are nevertheless still together. They might have all forsaken Jesus in the Garden of Gethsemane and fled, but they did not scatter.

Over the previous months and years they had formed bonds with one another that survived the disappointment and disillusionment of the crucifixion. And while there are individual appearances of the risen Jesus, to Mary Magdalene and to Peter, most of the resurrection appearances are to groups of disciples: to the Eleven, to the seven by the Sea of Tiberias, and, Paul says, to more than five hundred of the brethren at once. These are shared experiences, uniting this band of followers ever more closely with one another and with their Lord and Saviour.

It is no surprise then to find, as we begin to read the stories of the Early Church in the book of Acts, that there is considerable emphasis on the mutual fellowship of the first believers. They are gathered together in the upper room as they wait for the coming of the Holy Spirit, and that is how the Spirit finds them on the Day of Pentecost: all together in one place (Acts 2.1). The earliest description that we have of the life of the early church is found in Acts 2.42-47:

> *They devoted themselves to the apostles teaching and to the fellowship, to the breaking of bread and to prayer. Everyone was filled with awe, and many miraculous signs were done by the apostles. All the believers were together and had everything*

> *in common. Selling their possessions and goods, they gave to anyone as he had need. Every day they continued to meet together in the temple courts. They broke bread in their homes and ate together with glad and sincere hearts, praising God and enjoying the favour of all the people. And the Lord added to their number daily those who were being saved.*

Three times in three verses it is said that the believers were together: in the temple, in their homes and just, all together. They always seem to be together, and this, as much as anything else, seems to be what draws others to join them.

The Greek word that describes this togetherness is *koinonia.* It is a difficult word to translate. 'Community' in English, is a word that has been overused and can now mean something or nothing. *Koinonia* is translated as 'fellowship' in verse 42 but that word has become too churchy (though for want of a better one I shall continue to use it in this book).

'Friendship' is in many ways a better word. It is a good word for our relationships as Christians. Jesus said, 'I have called you friends' (John

15.15). Yet fellowship is more than mere friendship. Perhaps the word 'fellowship' has been partially rescued by Tolkien's book and film *The Fellowship of the Ring*. This at least demonstrates that fellowship is friendship with a focus or a common goal. The focus of our Christian friendships is our common friendship with Jesus and our common goal is his Kingdom.

Koinonia means 'sharing life together' or 'living a common life.' In our case: the life of the Kingdom of God. It is often remarked that the New Testament provides almost no information about the institutional structures of the early church, and indeed such information as we have suggests that these structures were fluid and adaptable. Neither Jesus nor the Apostles thought it necessary to provide the church with a constitution.

This vagueness has been the source of division over the centuries between the institutional churches. But it should serve to remind us that at its heart the church has always been and should always be, not an institution, but a fellowship. The ties that bind us together are not supposed to be institutional ones, but the ties of friendship and fellowship, of love. The official title of the

Quakers is 'The Society of Friends.' It would or should make a good title for every church. But it is also a challenge: are we really friends with one another?

Koinonia was used as a word to describe a common life not just by the early church but by other groups of people in the ancient Greek and Roman world, often with the same connotation of a sharing of worldly goods and pursuing mutual interests. In our own culture, it might have been used about a Rotary Club or a Masonic Lodge (complete with its occult ritual ceremonies) or even about the Branch of a Trades Union. But the fellowship of the church, compared with that of other societies in the ancient world, had certain distinctive features.

Most societies of this sort, then and now, consist of people drawn from the same social class: Rotary is generally a dining club of professional people in the town; the Masonic Lodge is usually a coterie of local business people; a Trades Union Branch is essentially an association of people in the same trade. But the *koinoia* of the church, embraced equally masters and slaves, sometimes masters and their own slaves (Philemon 16). This was unprecedented in the ancient world, where the deepest social division of all was that between bond and free.

A remarkable feature of the church, and one that perhaps caused even more comment, was that it embraced both men and women. Men and women were baptised with the same rites; they partook equally in the common meals; and the women as well as the men enjoyed a remarkable freedom to pray and to prophesy in the meetings, even if Paul insisted that the women should cover their heads. Sometimes the wife even seemed to be the more prominent member of a couple than the husband, for example Priscilla and Aquila (Rom 16.3).

This is not to enter into contemporary arguments about women in authority in the church, but simply to point out the extraordinary position that was accorded to women in the early Christian fellowship, compared to their status in contemporary society. In the ancient world, in both Jewish and Gentile culture, women were considered to be altogether inferior to men. The Jewish attitude to women is summed up in the words with which the Pharisee used to bless himself, 'I thank thee, O Lord, that thou hast not made me a woman.'

Paul might have been uncomfortable with the idea of a woman teaching, but the rabbis were uncomfortable with the idea of a woman learning: 'Sooner let the words of the Law be burnt than delivered to women,' said one of them.

One of the unique things about Jesus as a Jewish Teacher was that he was as happy to have a woman sitting at his feet and listening as a man (Luke 10.39). This freedom was equally typical of the church (provided that the women did not chat during the sermon; 1 Corinthians 14.34-35). No wonder Christianity appealed to women; the surprise, perhaps, is that it continued to appeal no less to men.

There are even clues that the fellowship of the church embraced differences of race. On the road from Jerusalem to Gaza, very early in the history of the church, Philip fell in with an Ethiopian, an African, to whom he preached the gospel and whom he baptised (Acts 8.26-39).

Later in Antioch we find, alongside a Palestinian aristocrat like Manaen, one Simeon, whose soubriquet suggests that he also was black (Acts 13.1). Thus the fellowship of the apostolic church drew together people from across all the divisions of the ancient, and modern, world: divisions of class, gender and race.

The fellowships of the ancient world were often associated with the mystery religions and religious cults, with their secret ceremonies of initiation and membership, just like the Freemasons today. The Christian church was equally clearly a religious fellowship but its rites and ceremonies were open and often public. The only times in the early church when Christians practised their worship in secret were during periods of persecution. Otherwise, baptisms were often conducted in public places, as on the Day of Pentecost (Acts 2.41), or in the sight of anyone who happened to be passing by (Acts 8.38).

The Christians never made any secret of what happened in their meetings. And while the Christians certainly fulfilled all the characteristics of a religious group, their fellowship also transcended that other profound division of the ancient world, the religious division between Jew and Greek. Nothing except a thorough-going change of heart would have persuaded a Jew to sit down and eat with a Gentile (Acts 10).

Another aspect of this new religious fellowship was that its adherents' excluded themselves from any other religious affiliation or observance. This was equally strange, and often obnoxious to their contemporaries, as it is sometimes strange and obnoxious to ours. Christians would not join in the pagan festivals and orgies, nor with the acts of ritual homage to the Roman Emperor.

This would later bring them into conflict with the Roman authorities, as well as into bad odour with their neighbours who considered them, no doubt, bigoted and intolerant. And yet their exclusivity, like that of the Jews, out of whose synagogues they had sprung, was one of the fascinations of this strange new fellowship.

An unmissable feature of this fellowship is that it involved a radical sharing of goods and money. From the beginning in Jerusalem, 'All the believers had everything in common. Selling their possessions and goods, they gave to anyone as he had need.' Nor was this a flash in the pan. In a more extended passage, Acts 4.32-37, details are given of how this worked and of an individual, Barnabas, who sold a field and brought the money and 'put it at the apostles' feet.

Such giving away of personal wealth for the common good was not compulsory, but remained a free-will gesture of love towards other, needier members of the fellowship. The next incident in the book of Acts makes this clear. Ananias and his wife Sapphira conspired together to get the credit for such an act of generosity whilst actually keeping some of the money back for themselves (Acts 5.1-11).

Peter's rebuke reveals that the couple were not obliged to sell their property in the first place, nor, having sold it, were they obliged to give the whole of the proceeds to the church. Their fault lay in lying about their generosity to the church and to the Holy Spirit. They both dropped dead!

We see here also the mechanism for the distribution of these common funds. Monies such as this were 'put at the apostles' feet.' Very soon the business of administering the common funds proved too onerous for the Twelve and it was necessary to select seven other men to undertake this work, while the apostles concentrated on the ministry of the word and prayer (Acts 6.1-6).

The chief category of beneficiary of this distribution was the widows. Thirty years later, when Paul is writing to Timothy, the same sort of system still seems to be working in the fellowship of the churches in Ephesus, a predominantly Gentile church (1 Timothy 5.9-16).

By this time the church was encountering all the usual problems of administering benefits or relief to poor people: some widows were abusing the system, presuming on the generosity of the fellowship rather than taking steps to help themselves, and some families were abdicating their own responsibilities for their relatives on the assumption that the church would take care of them. Even this testifies to the continuance of a spirit of mutual care and support for one another that, in spite of abuses, still animated the fellowship of the church.

Such sharing also characterised relations between churches, as well as within churches. One of Paul's earliest visits to Jerusalem, some fourteen years after his conversion, was occasioned by the commission of the church in Antioch to take to the church in Jerusalem an offering to relieve the sufferings of the Christians in Judea, as the result of a famine (Acts 11.27-30). Later, Paul organised a major collection of gifts for the poor of Jerusalem from amongst all the churches that he had founded in Asia Minor,

Macedonia and Greece (1 Corinthians 16.1-4). It was in the process of delivering this collection that he was arrested in Jerusalem and sent on his final journey in the book of Acts, as a prisoner to Rome.

150 years later, Tertullian could describe the fellowship of the Christians in Carthage in North Africa in terms that are recognisably similar to those in the book of Acts (in his *Apologetica, ch. 39*, around 200 AD). The care for one another expressed in the sharing of goods is still a feature of the common life:

> *Each puts in a small donation; but only if it be his pleasure, and only if he be able: for there is no compulsion; all is voluntary. These gifts are, as it were, piety's deposit fund. For they are not taken thence and spent on feasts, and drinking-bouts, and eating-houses, but to support and bury poor people, to supply the wants of boys and girls destitute of means and parents, and of old persons confined now to the house; such, too, as have suffered shipwreck; and if there happen to be any in the mines, or banished*

> *to the islands, or shut up in the prisons, for nothing but their fidelity to the cause of God's Church, they become the nurslings of their confession.*

The Christians, Tertullian says, regard each other as brothers and sisters in the same family:

> *How much more fittingly they are called and counted brothers who have been led to the knowledge of God as their common Father, who have drunk in one Spirit of holiness, who from the same womb of a common ignorance have agonized into the same light of truth. One in mind and soul, we do not hesitate to share our earthly goods with one another. All things are common among us except our wives.*

The mixed nature of Christian gatherings was a constant source of suspicion in the secular world outside the fellowship. Many of the fellowship groups to which the Romans were accustomed to belong involved sexual licence, either as part of their religious rituals or in association with drunken orgies. Exclusively male as they were, like the local rugby club, their idea of letting their hair down together usually involved a lot of alcohol and women. Naturally, the world outside suspected that the same things went on amongst the Christians. What else would they want women for? Tertullian contradicted these suspicions on every count:

> *Our feast explains itself by its name. The Greeks call it agapè, i.e., affection. Whatever it costs, our outlay in the name of piety is gain, since with the good things of the feast we benefit the needy; nor as it is with you, do parasites aspire to the glory of satisfying their licentious propensities, selling themselves for a belly-feast to all disgraceful treatment—but as it is with God himself, a peculiar respect is shown to the lowly. As it is an act of religious service, it permits no vileness or immodesty. The participants, before reclining, taste first of prayer to God. As much is eaten as satisfies the cravings of hunger; as much is drunk as befits the chaste. They say it is enough, as those who remember that even during the night they have to worship God; they talk as*

> *those who know that the Lord is one of their auditors. As the feast commenced with prayer, so with prayer it is closed. We go from it, not like troops of mischief-doers, nor bands of vagabonds, nor to break out into licentious acts, but to have as much care of our modesty and chastity as if we had been at a school of virtue rather than a banquet.*

Indeed Tertullian goes on to show that far from tolerating licentious behaviour, the elders of the church are diligent in disciplining any who err in this direction:

> *We are a body knit together as such by a common religious profession, by unity of discipline, and by the bond of a common hope. We meet together as an assembly and congregation, that, offering up prayer to God as with united force, we may wrestle with Him in our supplications. We assemble to read our sacred writings. With the sacred words we nourish our faith, we animate our hope, we make our confidence more steadfast; and no less by*

inculcations of God's precepts we confirm good habits. In the same place also exhortations are made, rebukes and sacred censures are administered. For with a great gravity is the work of judging carried on among us, as befits those who feel assured that they are in the sight of God; and you have the most notable example of judgment to come when any one has sinned so grievously as to require his severance from us in prayer, in the congregation and in all sacred intercourse.

These last remarks reveal two things about the fellowship of the early church at the end of the second century, both of which can also be seen in the life of the church in apostolic times.

Firstly, the church through its elders or leaders exercised a discipline over its members, the purpose of which was both to rebuke and correct the individual and also to protect the integrity and purity of the fellowship. We shall have more to say about such discipline in a subsequent chapter. But the second thing that Tertullian reveals is that the fellowship of the church was not perfect. He paints a favorable picture of the life together of the early Christians, but he does not pretend that there were not faults that did not, from time to time, need to be rebuked and corrected.

This is plain even in the pages of the New Testament. Much of Paul's correspondence was penned in order to correct faults that were developing in these infant congregations. In Corinth there were factions forming around various teachers, Paul, Apollos, Peter, and those tiresomely smug individuals who claimed to be above denominational allegiances and 'only followed Christ.'

There was one particularly glaring case of sexual immorality within the congregation in Corinth, but there were also lawsuits going on between church members, and believers resorting to prostitutes. The *agapé,* or common meal, for which the church gathered and during which they commemorated the death and resurrection of Jesus with the breaking of bread and the drinking of wine, was being spoiled by greed and drunkenness. The prayers and the singing were prone to confusion as people prophesied and spoke in tongues without reference to others.

The whole thing sounds unbelievably appalling. No wonder that Paul found the daily pressure of his care for all the churches as great a burden as the imprisonments, floggings and dangers that he often faced (2 Corinthians 11.28). Yet, through the grace and power of God, these early churches did not disintegrate into disagreement and dissoluteness, but continued to meet together and actually grew.

In spite of everything, these Christians had a message of astoundingly good news to proclaim, and although too much of the old nature still remained in them, there was also irrefutable evidence in their lives, both as individuals and as a fellowship, of a new nature and a new power to transform human beings and their life together, that no other religion or philosophy could offer.

Paul and the other apostles never gave up exhorting these fellowships of new Christians to persevere in their love for one another, to forgive one another, to be kind and forbearing to one another, and to live lives that were holy and pleasing to their God and worthy of their Lord and Saviour Jesus Christ. And it worked: in spite of all the Christians' shortcomings, the Word of God and the Spirit of God went on transforming individuals more and more into the likeness of Christ, and their life together continued to form one of the principle attractions that drew unbelievers to join them.

According to Tertullian, 150 years after the time of Paul, it was the pagans who said of the Christians, '*See how they love one another*,' and they were not joking.

Chapter Five

FOSTERING FELLOWSHIP:
THE FOUNTAIN OF LIFE

How do we foster such fellowship in the church today? The first thing to be said is that we cannot create for ourselves the sort of fellowship about which we read in the early church; it was, and is, the work of the Holy Spirit.

It is no coincidence that the description of the life of the first believers in Jerusalem, that we read about in Acts 2.42-47, is the climax of the story of the Day of Pentecost. It is the outpouring of the Holy Spirit that leads to this life together. When Paul is signing off at the end of the second letter to the Corinthians, he commends the Christians to the grace of the Lord Jesus Christ, the love of God, and the fellowship of the Holy Spirit. It is this sharing in the fellowship of the Holy Spirit that is the foundation of the fellowship of the church.

Paul is clear that the sort of love that we experience in the church is a supernatural love rather than a natural one: 'God has poured out his love into our hearts by the Holy Spirit, whom he has given us' (Romans 5.5). Our natural loves are reserved for those who are like us in some way: our families, our husbands and wives, our children, our friends, our fellow countrymen, our own race, those who share our culture or upbringing. This new love enables us to love those who are unlike us, as we have seen in the fellowship of the early church. This love is the fruit of the Spirit (Galatians 5.22). 1 Corinthians 13, despite its appropriation for use at weddings and all sorts of other vaguely religious occasions, is primarily about life in the Spirit. Love is the over-riding and controlling attitude with which we are to exercise the gifts of the Spirit.

1 Corinthians 13-type love is not love as we know it in everyday life: 'It is patient and kind. It does not envy, it does not boast, it is not proud. It is not rude, it is not self-seeking, it is not easily angered, it keeps no record of wrongs.' It is the love of God for us, a love in which we are invited to share in our love for one another.

'You yourselves have been taught by God to love each other,' Paul says (1 Thessalonians 4.10). 'Yet,' he goes on, 'we urge you, brothers, to do so more and more.' As with all the gifts and fruit of the Spirit, while we may experience these things spontaneously as we are filled with the Holy Spirit, we nevertheless have to cultivate and foster them. This is because the old nature or 'the flesh' in us is not yet dead.

We live with the tension of the old nature at war with the new nature within us. So we have continually to mortify or put to death the old nature and at the same time cultivate and foster the things that belong to the new nature, including that love that forms between us the fellowship or common life of the church.

The centrality of this loving fellowship to the Christian life is emphasised by the frequency with which Paul and the other apostles return to it in their letters. 'I pray that your love may abound more and more' (Philippians 1.9). 'Dear friends, let us love one another' (1 John 4.7). 'Over all these virtues put on love, which binds them all together in perfect unity' (Colossians 3.14). Love for one another is both a gift of the Holy Spirit poured into our hearts, but also something that we need to preserve and foster.

* * *

I want to look now at the life of two churches today that have experienced the outpouring of the Holy Spirit and the new life that the Spirit brings, and which have deliberately fostered such love between their members. In each case this fostering of loving friendship has been associated with significant growth in the church and a remarkable quality of fellowship.

The first of these churches is the Fountain of Life Church, Norfolk. This new Anglican church grew out of two country parishes that began to experience the renewal of the gifts of the Holy Spirit in the late 1980s. Today the Fountain of Life has an adult membership of around 250.

In traditional churches, like those in the two original villages, church fellowship is focused on Sunday services: it is by coming to church on Sundays that people feel that they belong to the church, and it is there that they get to know one another. But this sort of fellowship inevitably remains at a superficial level.

Fostering fellowship in the church requires opportunities to spend more time together than an hour on Sunday mornings, and to share our lives, our faith and our perplexities, our joys and sorrows, at a deeper level.

From the beginning, fellowship in the Apostolic church was fostered both in meeting together in the temple courts, and in meeting in each other's houses (Acts 2.46). I believe that at all times the church has needed to meet in these two ways, and in times of its vitality it always has: meeting as a congregation on a Sunday and meeting in smaller groups in houses in the week.

As churches grow, as the Fountain of Life has done, the Sunday services become more in the nature of celebrations. There are too many people for anyone to know more than a fraction of the congregation, as must have been the case in Jerusalem at the beginning when 3000 were baptised in a single day. For the purposes of fellowship and friendship the meetings in each other's houses assume the greater importance.

In the Fountain of Life, membership of a home group has never been compulsory, but over 80% of the church members also belong to a home group. I undertook a survey in 2010 amongst the members of this church to enquire about their experience of friendship or fellowship in the church, and to find out more about how fellowship has been fostered in the church.

In a sample of eighty people of all ages, seventy-seven (96%) said that they had friends in the church. Most claimed to have made 'many', 'lots', or 'loads' of friends. One eighty-two year-old, replied, 'Yes,' she had made friends, 'those who bring me by car, those who now look after me, and many who come and talk to me while I wait to be taken home.'

When asked what they appreciated most about the church, amongst such responses as Bible teaching, freedom in worship, and a church for all the family, fifty-four mentioned the groups to which they belonged, and the friendship or fellowship that they had found. One fourteen year-old replied, 'It feels safe, like a second home', and a sixty year-old simply said that she most appreciated the love.

Asked how and where these friendships had been formed and nourished, the respondents were given the choices of:

- Sunday mornings over coffee (served in the middle of the service)
- In a home group
- Through being invited to meals in other people's homes

- Through working together as part of a church team
- Through other church social activities or courses.

83% of friendships were cultivated over Sunday morning coffee, 70% in home groups, 70% over meals in each other's houses, 63% through working in a church team and 66% through other church activities and courses, such as Alpha.

People were asked whether anyone had spoken to them the first time that they came to church. There is a team of people each Sunday who stand at the door of the church specifically to welcome everyone, so it is difficult to come in at all without at least saying 'good morning' and shaking someone's hand. But many of the respondents in the survey obviously understood the question to mean more than this. 93% said someone had spoken to them the first time they came to the church. Only one replied, 'No'; the other 6% had been part of the church from the beginning or had grown up in the church from infancy.

Further questions asked if people had received either practical or financial help from other members of the church. Many people had received some sort of practical help, ranging from the loan of clothes or tools, help with gardening and trees, fixing the car and electrical problems, bringing in meals and gifts of food, child care, shopping, help with moving house, lifts to everywhere from airports to surgeries, and even Christian friends coming in to live with single people after discharge from hospital.

Perhaps more surprisingly 15% had at some time received financial help from other members of the fellowship. I suspect that most of these deeds of kindness and compassion are unknown to the church leadership and certainly not organised by anyone officially, but are simply expressions of love for one another.

Fred and Carol, and Simon and Becca, are amongst the people who lead home groups in the church. Simon and Becca's group is made up of around fifteen twenty-somethings, while Fred and Carol have a similar number of more middle-aged people. Both groups have a weekly evening meeting in someone's house. At the beginning people arrive and, over a drink and a nibble, chat about everyday matters, work, family, church.

Fred and Carol work to a ten-week plan that alternates bible study, worship, prayer and social activities, while Simon and Becca follow a published series of notes including a bible reading and topical questions for discussion. Both groups have an active social life, including meals together, picnics and parties, outings to concerts, cinemas, theatres, and bowling.

Simon and Becca's group have an annual day out on the Norfolk Broads, while Fred and Carol have taken their group on holiday to Paris and Bruges. Other evenings are spent playing games or having quizzes. Social outings and evenings are opportunities to invite non-Christian family and friends.

The friendships formed amongst the younger people in particular lead to many practical ways of helping each other: building a new fence, help with moving house, or looking after the cats. When Julia had a major car accident and was immobilised for several weeks, it was friends from Simon and Becca's group who looked after her while her husband went to work, shopping, cooking meals, and washing up.

After finishing at university, Becca had wondered if she would ever be able to make such close friendships again. But she has found an even closer bond with the members of the Home Group that she and her husband were asked to lead.

Two of the members of this group are Matt and Harriet. They had just finished at university, had fallen in love, and as young Christians were anxious to marry. But how to find and set up a first home? In the providence of God they were offered a new, shared-equity, maisonette by the local Housing Association. But how to furnish it? This is Matt's story:

> *In the run up to my wedding I had spent the year working for my church as an unpaid intern. My future wife was completing her teacher training course. We had no money, or rather, we had a lot of student debt, and I was due to move into our first home 3 months before the big day. We had no idea how I was to live or how we would furnish the house before we were married. With a mixture of help from friends and family, especially in the*

church, in the end furnishing the house cost my wife and me £15. Here is a list of the gifts that we received.

- *Two sofas*
- *One double-bed*
- *A set of drawers and a matching cupboard*
- *A book case*
- *A desk*
- *A fridge freezer*
- *Cooking utensils*
- *A microwave*
- *Coffee tables*
- *A kettle and drink making facilities*
- *£700 to carpet the house (with enough left to buy a washing machine!)*
- *Our rent paid up until the first month of our marriage*

The £15 of our own that we spent bought us a second hand gas cooker, which still works perfectly fine. In the period of time running up to our wedding and immediately after we received many more gifts and much more money from our church family and were thoroughly touched by their generosity. We thank God for these gifts and his provision through his church and as a married couple we wish to live a generous life joyfully giving as God calls us to.

At the other end of life, Jean became increasingly infirm in mind as well as in body, and came to rely more and more on friends in the congregation, first to bring her to church on Sundays and then for all her daily needs. Jean was a spinster, her only relatives being a niece and nephews with whom she had had little contact all her life and who lived many miles away.

David, a retired bank manager, and his wife Christine, and another friend in the church, Susan, took her under their wing. It was David and Christine who started to bring Jean to church on Sundays, but it was Susan who took on the main responsibility for caring for Jean's other needs. As time went on, Jean needed more and more help with cooking and cleaning, washing and dressing, shopping, taking her medication, and managing her finances.

David, as an ex-bank-manager, took Jean's financial affairs in hand. This had to be done with extreme delicacy and caution, involving consultations with doctors, lawyers, and social workers, as well as the niece and nephews, who were pleased that people locally were willing to take on responsibility for their aged aunt. Eventually a Power of Attorney was drawn up and registered with the Court of Protection, giving David discretion and power to act for Jean.

Meanwhile, Susan negotiated step by step with Social Services for Jean to receive the assistance of paid carers. Susan herself put in many hours of unpaid time in taking Jean to the shops and keeping her company at home. Various tradesmen in the church, an electrician, a plumber and a decorator came in to sort out Jeans' central heating, her kitchen and her bathroom and charged her a minimal amount.

At last, Jean's mind deteriorated to the point where she needed full-time residential care in a home for the elderly mentally infirm. Susan, David and Christine found a suitable residential place for her and helped her with the transition out of her own home into this strange environment. They visited Jean in the home and later in the hospital where she ended her days.

At no point did David and Christine or Susan receive any financial reward for all the love and care that they showed to Jean. They had no formal responsibility for her; only the love of God, poured out into their hearts, compelled them to look after this sister in the Lord. Susan had known Jean for many years before her infirmity and knew that, even in her better days, she had a difficult temperament. But the Lord assured Susan that the yoke would be easy and the burden light. And so, by his grace, it proved to be. Fellowship can be costly, but as Susan has said, 'A real close friendship formed between Jean and me, and I received as many blessings as I gave. In the words of St Francis, "It is in giving that we receive."'

Jean is the sort of person who could easily have ended up on the crematorium rota as, '*No mourners. No minister required.*' Thanks to her Christian friends, Jean was loved and cared for through her last days and had a joyful and hearty send-off in her own church.

There have been other aspects of the life of the Fountain of Life Church that it has shared with many other churches in UK and throughout the world, but which have contributed to the growth of fellowship amongst the congregation.

The well-known Alpha course has been so successful that it has spread to over 163 countries and is used by thousands of churches of all denominations world-wide. The name is used as a mnemonic for the course:

A for anyone
L for learning and laughter
P for plenty of food
H for helping one another
A for ask anything

Alpha provides people with basic instruction in the Christian faith, an opportunity to explore the meaning of life, and fellowship or friendship with others on the same journey. Much social life at all levels, from the family, to the gym, to the place of work, to the bar, takes place at a very superficial level - 'How's things, mate?' 'Fine.' - when in reality 'things' are often tough, relationships are bad, and there is an emptiness inside that nothing seems to fill.

Alpha is successful partly because it gives people the opportunity to talk about their lives as they really are and to explore the big questions that life asks of us all. It does so in a convivial and relaxing environment in which a main ingredient is food. Alpha is often the first time that people have found the love and acceptance that enables them to open up and talk about their lives, their disappointments and failures, their beliefs and perplexities, without fear of scorn and rejection.

Many churches find that friendships formed on Alpha continue after the course is over, either because the group continues as a church home group, or because those involved voluntarily go on meeting together informally. People do not only need answers to their questions, they also need company as they search for them. Alpha helps them to find both; it is more than a course, it is a fellowship.

It has been pointed out that there are three elements to the Christian life: believing, behaving and belonging. There is a temptation for churches to require people to behave before they belong. In fact the order for most people becoming Christians, and perhaps the correct Gospel order, is for outsiders to be welcomed into some expression of the fellowship of the church, where they learn to believe, and, after their conversion, begin to put their lives in order. This is certainly the more typical way in which Alpha works: belong, believe, behave.

New Wine started in 1989 as a week's summer family conference. These weeks have proliferated both in the UK and in other countries. They are similar to Christian conferences organised by other churches or networks of churches either for their own members or for the wider Christian public.

An important, but often overlooked, aspect of New Wine is that it involves people, not just worshipping together, sharing teaching and receiving ministry in the power of the Holy Spirit, but also camping and caravanning together – in all weathers! Groups of people from the Fountain of Life Church have spent a week together at New Wine since the beginning in 1989, at first a small group of nine, later as many as sixty. That meant that over the years the church became a fellowship of people, many of whom had camped together and shared both the joys and the hardships of the English summer.

From the point of view of building fellowship it does not seem to matter what the weather brings, though of course the experience is pleasanter in the sunshine. There is a special sort of joy that is found sitting together around a table or a barbecue in the twilight, with the children tucked up in their tents, talking and laughing together on a warm summer's evening until the stars come out.

But even a week spent together wrestling with tents that are blowing away or with cars that are bogged down in the mud, builds fellowship and a sense of comradeship in adversity. Either way, these are times of listening to one another, praying for one another, helping one another, and deepening relationships in a way that is impossible in the occasional hours spent together in church or at home.

Over the years, groups from the church have made pilgrimages together. Since the Middle Ages and Chaucer's *Canterbury Tales*, pilgrimages have been a way of combining a holiday with a spiritual purpose. A pilgrimage to the Holy Land, difficult as this is today with the present state of enmity and division between Israelis and Palestinians, is a wonderful way, both to deepen our understanding of the Bible and its background, and to share together in a profound and moving spiritual experience.

All these times spent together, whether in serious attention to God's Word or in playing charades, meeting on a winter's evening at someone's house or camping together in a muddy field, catching up with each other over coffee on a Sunday morning or praying together in the Garden of Gethsemane, these are the ingredients of fellowship, in which love for one another has been birthed and fostered in the Fountain of Life Church.

Chapter Six

FOSTERING FELLOWSHIP:
HILLSONG CHURCH, LONDON

Coming up out of the London Underground at Tottenham Court Road, you are face to face with the Dominion Theatre. All the week the theatre shows some lavish musical, but during Saturday night it is transformed into a church. This is the meeting place of Hillsong Church, London.

For about twelve hours on a Sunday there is a continuous stream of mostly young people coming and going through the doors. Nearly 10,000 people will attend one of the four services. This church was only founded in 1999 from the parent church in Sydney, Australia. Within a few years it grew to 500, then to 5,000, and now to its present size. By English standards the growth has been phenomenal, and it still continues.

What is the secret of this church growth? Some might point to the music. The stage of the theatre is set up as if for a pop concert, there is a band, half-a-dozen singers, a worship leader, ever changing lights, huge screens. The thump of the bass drum resonates not just in the ears but in every organ of the body. But this is worship, songs of praise, adoration and commitment to Jesus. Every member of the band means every word they sing and play, and, unlike a pop concert, the audience or congregation are singing with them. If Christians around the world have heard of Hillsong, it is probably for their songs, many written by their own singers and worship-leaders. The worship is vibrant, exciting and loud! But there is something much more to Hillsong than the joy and razzmatazz of their worship: there is love.

I was having lunch at Starbucks, just round the corner in New Oxford Street, before visiting the church for the first time. At the same small table was a tired and somewhat dishevelled black woman. She was joined briefly by a middle-aged white woman, who brought her food and drink that she had bought for her at the counter.

After a while the black woman at our table inquired of my wife and me: 'You goin' to Hillsong?' I said that we were. 'Most folks in here are goin' to Hillsong,' she said, 'I'm goin' myself when I eat this. I'm on a Host team there. But I been workin' and when I turn up, I had a funny turn. So that lady, she my team leader, she say, "You need somethin' to eat, give you some strength." So she brought me round here and get me this food. That's why I go to Hillsong: they love each one. Don't matter who you is, rich or poor, you come as you are, and they love you – one by one.'

Before she left to go back to her duties at the theatre, my new friend introduced me to Dez, a young man wearing a Hillsong badge who had also been eating at Starbucks. 'Dez'll tell you 'bout Hillsong,' she said. Dez was Brazilian. He had come to London to study and work and had found himself friendless and alone in the great city. He had fallen in with some other young Brazilians but he had not liked their life-style and had heard of Hillsong as a friendly church. Coming from a Christian background in Brazil, he had joined Hillsong and was now the leader of the international ministry team. He also had to be going to fulfil his role in the church, so we walked back to the theatre together. 'Everyone is known by name,' he said, 'we try to love each other, one by one.'

At the entrance to the foyer there were other young people, identified by their Hillsong jackets, speaking to everyone who came through the doors. Inside the foyer there were more young people available to help anyone who looked lost or questioning. One of these quickly enabled me to identify and find Shaun, my contact at the church. Together we went up to the balcony where we were given coffee and where we could talk.

All the time a tide of young people flowed in and out of the auditorium, leaving one service and making their way in to the next. How could anyone keep in touch with this multitude enough to know and care for each one?

It is not only a matter of numbers, but of the sheer transience of London's population. London is today perhaps the most cosmopolitan city in the world. People from every corner of the globe inhabit its streets, its shops, its offices, its pleasure domes. It is not so much the ethnic ghettoes that exist in London that are so amazing; it is the people of every race and colour, of every language and nationality, standing on the Tube and walking down the streets, shoulder to shoulder, all mixed up together in one extraordinary melting pot. London has always been one of the great cities of the Earth, (I grew up there, so I know). But in the 21st century, all the world has come to London and all the world seems to love it.

But there is nothing as impersonal as a crowd. Someone arriving in London, whether from Japan or from the English provinces, can feel bewildered and isolated. Where do I start to make friends and find a life for myself here? There is a superficial life-style of clubs, pubs, drinking, drugs and sex, that can be accessed everywhere, and which seems to offer the warmth of companionship and love. But it is a sham. It is more likely to lead to trouble and shame than to happiness and peace. Many young people in London and elsewhere are looking for something else, and Hillsong has got it: a relationship with God and love for one another. But how does it work?

Hillsong uses every technical and electronic assistance that the 21st century can offer to further its work and mission. This is apparent on the stage during the times of worship as much as in the data-bases of phone numbers and e-mail addresses. Yet these are not the secret of the church's growth and success. If every computer crashed and every data-base were lost, Hillsong would carry on. This is a church that depends above all on the personal relationships that its members have with one another. These personal relationships are the invisible ropes that connect and hold the church together. It may seem a tenuous way to run a mega-church, but it works.

Sunday, for all the genuineness of the warmth and the welcome is only the tip of the iceberg. Most of the ongoing life of the church is out of sight. Sunday worship may be a powerful experience but there must be a different sort of glue that holds the people together.

The Sunday congregations look like the audiences that throng the Dominion Theatre every other night of the week. But those audiences disperse and have no further contact with one another; they are not friends when they come and they are not friends when they leave. They have shared a theatrical experience but that is their only connection. It might appear that Sunday services at Hillsong are the same. But they are not.

In the foyer are banners that say, 'Welcome Home. The heart and soul of Hillsong Church is to introduce and connect people with the living God.' The banner might add, 'and to connect them with one another', for it invites you to 'Connect Me.' During the service there will be an opportunity to make a connection with the living God through his Son Jesus Christ, or to reconnect with this God if you have been away. If you put up a hand, someone will come alongside you and offer you a Bible and suggest how you might take the next step in your journey with God.

On each chair as the worshippers take their seats is a welcome pack. If you are new to the church, you are invited to fill in your name and contact details. Someone from the church will call you during the week and suggest different ways of becoming connected to others in Hillsong.

Church teams are taught not to put pressure on people at any point but to give them space to make their own decisions and connections. At the end of every service the banners in the foyer serve as assembly points for anyone new to the church who wants to meet others or find out more about the church. Team members will take them out in twos and threes to a coffee bar or a restaurant to get to know them and to introduce them to one another.

After that there are two fundamental ways of staying connected: Connect Groups and Volunteer Teams, and these are at the heart of how fellowship and friendship are fostered in Hillsong. Connect Groups are small: eight is regarded as the optimum size. They meet weekly or fortnightly in hundreds of places in and around London, sometimes in homes, sometimes in coffee houses or restaurants.

Their time together usually includes four ingredients: welcome, food, study and prayer. Connect Groups have a host or leader. The host is not the teacher but the convenor and the pastor of the group. Each week Connect Group leaders are encouraged to download a Bible study from the church website that will be linked to the previous Sunday's sermon. This study will be shared with the group, with the maximum opportunity given for discussion and response. A group may well agree to meet at other times in the week for social activities, going to films, or even holidays together.

The church provides centralised courses for new Christians, called Discovering Christianity, and more challenging opportunities for further study at its Evening College. But Connect Groups are the places where everyone grows in their understanding of God and of the practices of living the Christian life.

Hillsong Church relies heavily on Volunteer Teams. With a salaried staff of only forty people, most of the work in the church is done by volunteers. The teams are responsible for everything, from setting up the sound and vision equipment on the stage to playing in the band, from serving coffee to welcoming visitors at the door, from leading a Connect Group to offering counselling and advice on the Care Team, from teaching children's groups to running the youth activities.

Every team has a leader and the teams meet together weekly, aside from their volunteering duties, and function as their own Connect Groups. Thus, each connected member of the church is in a small group with its own leader or pastor. The leader's primary responsibility is to know and care for each member of the group, being aware of any difficulties or problems someone may be facing, and supporting and helping them in any possible way. Teams in the church can provide specialist help with job-seeking, housing needs, debt and money management, or counselling for deeper emotional or relationship problems, but the first line of pastoral care is the Team or Connect Group leader.

The leaders themselves are accountable to and receive care from leaders of leaders. As well as monthly meetings as groups of leaders to talk about their own groups, each leader will have an individual meeting with their own leader of leaders to talk about their personal discipleship and walk with God. The church is a pyramid of leaders caring for other leaders, caring for their groups or teams.

There is a constant process of recruiting and appointing new leaders for connect Groups and Volunteer Teams. Each existing leader is responsible for identifying potential new leaders in their group. These potential leaders must be people of some personal and spiritual maturity. Over a period of weeks or months the leader will give such a person small areas of responsibility for the weekly meeting, to see how reliable and efficient they are. As the new leaders emerge the older ones will mentor and develop them into the role, until after, perhaps, a year they are ready to take over the responsibility for the group or to form a new one.

Chris had been brought up in a Christian home and had always had a relationship to God. He had asked Jesus to come into his life at his mother's knee and made a more mature commitment at a Christian youth event in his early teens. When he went to live in London as a university student it was natural that he should want to make a connection with a London church.

Chris and his parents had already worshipped at Hillsong on family visits to London, so a few weeks before his first term Chris e-mailed the church and asked to be put in touch. Within 24 hours, Shaun, my own contact there, had telephoned to welcome Chris and arrange a meeting. More than this, Shaun invited Chris to come and stay with him for a weekend.

Shaun spent a lot of time with Chris in his first term and introduced him to student Connect Groups. Chris was soon gathering his own Connect Group from amongst the people he was meeting at college. In Chris's hall of residence there was another young student, fresh to the university, called Daniel. The two were taking the same course and rapidly became friends. Daniel declared that he was an atheist, but was nevertheless intrigued that Chris spent most of his Sundays at church.

When Chris's Connect Group arranged a social outing together Chris invited Daniel to come along, and despite making it clear to everyone that he was an atheist Daniel made friends with the group and continued to attend their meetings, even when these involved prayer and bible study.

Curiosity must have got the better of him, because one day Daniel also asked if he could come to church with them on a Sunday. The celebration at the Dominion Theatre was not like anything that Daniel had ever experienced before. 'Was that church?' he asked, as they left the service. By the end of their first year Daniel had become a regular attender at both the Sunday services and the Connect Group meetings, at which Chris was now the leader.

Daniel was by nature quiet and reserved, and no one pressed him about the nature of his commitment, trusting that in his own time he would say what he wanted to say. As their first year of study was drawing to an end, these two friends decided to look for a flat to share together in their second year. The college's accommodation officer was interviewing them about their basic requirements: two bedrooms, their own kitchen and bathroom, and, said Daniel, 'a sitting room large enough for meetings of our Connect Group.'

At the beginning of his second year Chris found himself leading a Hillsong Connect Group of some 25 students. He himself was still being mentored by Shaun. During this year Daniel's father fell seriously ill and died. It was his Christian friends in the Connect Group and the church, especially Chris, who supported and encouraged him through this painful and distressing time. Chris had now become a mentor himself to others.

This is the structure that holds Hillsong together and makes it both a church and a place of real belonging. But the structure, vital as it is, is no more than a mould. Into this mould has to be poured the spirit of love for one another. That alone is what transforms the experience of belonging from a bureaucratic fiction, a name and a mobile phone number on a data base, into an experience of being known and valued.

Of course this spirit of love for one another depends on each member of the church, and especially the leaders at every level, practising what they preach. I had inadvertently witnessed this very thing on my first encounter with an ordinary member of Hillsong over the table at Starbucks. But even beyond that, this love must be God-inspired if it is to be more than a false smile and a patronising hand-out.

So, we are back to where we started with thinking about how to foster fellowship in the church: we cannot create for ourselves the sort of fellowship about which we read in the early church, or the love that Jesus urged us to have for one another. It was, and is, the work of the Holy Spirit.

* * *

What lessons can we learn from these two churches, the Fountain of Life Church in Norfolk and Hillsong Church in London, about fostering fellowship in the church? In many ways these two churches have very different origins.

Hillsong is a new church planted from scratch, with all the opportunities that offers for making a fresh start and designing the life of the church on a clean sheet. It operates within the busy, even frenetic, world of cosmopolitan London.

Fountain of Life, on the other hand, grew out of two traditional, Anglican, parish churches in the depths of the English countryside. Yet there are obvious similarities in the way that they have developed and in which they live their life as Christian congregations together. What can all churches learn then from these examples if we want our churches to be friendly, welcoming places, in which people of all sorts can find God and find the friendships and fellowship for which we were all created?

First, we need to look carefully at the Sunday gatherings of the whole church for worship. Are there people at the door to welcome everyone, friend and stranger alike?

It is important to choose the right people for this ministry, with open, smiling, faces, and the sensitivity to know whether a person wants to be greeted with the right hand of Christian fellowship, with a hug and a holy kiss, or simply with a friendly greeting. Such welcomers, except in the larger churches, should be people who know at least the majority of the congregation by sight and can therefore pick out the visitors and the new-comers and direct them to the right place to go.

In larger churches there needs to be a second wave of welcomers to whom strangers can refer for guidance and who will actually take people to a seat. There should be some sort of welcome pack available to give to new-comers, telling them a little about the church and inviting them to leave at least a name and number if they want to be contacted.

Holidays are a great opportunity for church-crawling, visiting different churches, perhaps of different denominations and traditions from our own, and it is always salutary to experience coming into a new church as a stranger. We can learn more about how to welcome and how not to welcome strangers in an hour in such a situation than we can learn in a life-time at home.

My wife and I always make a point of doing this on holiday wherever we may be. Many a time have we walked in and walked out of a church with no more than a distant nod and a mumbled word at the door. On the other hand we have been welcomed and shown to a seat, engaged in conversation by our neighbours, helped over practical difficulties, and been introduced to people who have shown a genuine interest in us and in our presence with them. Church Growth researchers found that people might go to a church once for all sorts of reasons, but they would only continue to go if they made friends. With those who simply come to see, we may have only one chance.

Many churches now serve coffee as an adjunct to the main service, before or after, which provides an opportunity to talk, both with those we know and with those we do not know. It is important to encourage the regular worshipers not to form cliques and ignore the stranger in their midst.

We all need to be reminded to make a point of introducing ourselves and talking to strangers. Some people in the congregation will have a special gift for this, but we all need to look at those around us in church with a view to identifying, not those we do know, but those we do not know.

When the Fountain of Life began to pause for coffee in the middle of the service there was a certain amount of grumbling about disturbing the worshipers' sense of the presence of God, or their concentration on the Word. But, as so often, it was only a matter of people forming new habits, and now the break for coffee in the middle is one of the most valued aspects of the service. Many Anglican and Catholic churches long ago introduced the liturgical custom of Sharing the Peace; a twenty-minute coffee break makes this a reality.

But closer and more sustained fellowship in the church requires meeting at other times in each others' homes or in smaller groups. Again, most charismatic churches have long had a structure of cells, house fellowships or home groups, to which people are encouraged to belong. The life of some of the new churches, like Hillsong, is structured around their cells or home groups rather than around their Sunday gatherings.

There are certain ingredients that are vital to the life of these home groups, but how these ingredients are mixed and served is infinitely varied. It is vital to read the Bible together and to pray together. These are the activities that sustained the lives of the believers in Jerusalem at the beginning (Acts 2.42): the teaching of the apostles and prayer.

In the smaller group we can be open and real with one another about our lives and our relationships; this is the place where Christian friends can pray specifically for each other's needs. Alongside teaching and prayer, meals together were apparently a constant feature of the common life of the early churches, meals that included the commemoration of the Lord's Supper, 'the breaking of bread.'

In modern church life, ordinary meals together and 'the breaking of bread' have usually become separated. This need not matter provided that both are part of our Christian life together somewhere, but it would be interesting to experience church life again where a meal and the Lord's Supper were regularly integrated as a regular part of the gathering. Hillsong do just that: Holy Communion is celebrated in their Connect Groups over common meals.

Home groups certainly ought to eat together in any case, and happy is the congregation that has the opportunity to eat together before or after a Sunday service. But alongside such organised meetings, church members should also be encouraged to invite one another to their homes *en famille.* It is in these places, where food is shared, that friendships and fellowship are formed.

Social activities without any sort of 'religious' agenda are also important ways of fostering the common life, and are opportunities to invite unsaved family, friends and neighbours to come and share that appetite for fun and the enjoyment of life that Christians should have in at least as great a measure as everyone else.

Walks in the country, bike rides, trips to the seaside or the swimming pool, outings to the bowling rink or the cinema, party-games and competitions, football matches and dances, holidays and camping: whatever we enjoy doing, let's do it together. Christian fellowship is not supposed to be intense or precious. We are supposed to be people who are naturally supernatural and supernaturally natural, which means that we can be both holy and lively, serious and light-hearted, committed and free, at the same time.

The fellowship of the Kingdom is not something in the end that can be organised or dictated from the top down. Structures are vital for the fostering of fellowship especially in the larger church, but there is no good looking to the structures or authorities of the church to tell us what to do to make friends with each other and enjoy ourselves together. The best children's games are those that the children improvise and organise for themselves. Interfering and bossy adults rarely make for lively and spirited children. It is the same in God's family.

The job of the church leaders or elders is to pick the right people to lead the home groups and then give them permission to be as imaginative and creative in their activities as they can. On the one hand, there are people in every church who would rule a home group with an iron hand for fear that someone might say or do something heretical or sinful; on the other hand, there are others who will constantly be devising new ways to stimulate bible study and enthuse the group with new ideas for reaching the lost.

One of the most important functions of church leaders at every level is to recognise the gifts that the Spirit is giving to people and to fit the ministry to the gift, and this applies especially to home group leaders.

It is out of friendships built up in a small group, sharing the things of God together, that the sharing of goods and possessions will naturally arise. Again, there may be a place for a congregation to hold a fund for the relief of individual financial need, or to organise a scheme for the supply of food or clothes or furniture to meet emergencies, but such sharing in material things will also arise freely and spontaneously where loving and caring relationships have been formed over a period of time in a house fellowship. There, we can know each other's needs, trust each other's integrity, and generously share what we have together, as in a family.

The fellowship of the Kingdom is a powerful attraction in a world that is characterised too much by loneliness and selfishness. A church that is open and welcoming to outsiders, that provides opportunities to make friends, and that offers a genuine mutuality of sharing, in things both spiritual and material, can expect to draw in many people who are deprived of love and meaning in their lives.

But now we must turn to the things that threaten to destroy the fellowship that we have so carefully built up. Paul not only urged believers in his churches to love one another, and to do so more and more, he also urged them to ‘keep the unity of the Spirit in the bond of peace’ (Ephesians 4.3).

Chapter Seven

KEEPING THE UNITY OF THE SPIRIT: 1

There are two sorts of issues that cause disunity in the church: personal issues and doctrinal issues. The first of these we shall look at in this chapter, the second in the next.

To live above with saints in love –
Ah! That will be glory.
To live below with saints we know –
Well, that's another story.

It is not easy to live together as sinful human beings in a fallen world, and it is not even easy to live together as beings who are being redeemed from their sinfulness in the church. For in this age our redemption is incomplete.

There is often a crisis in the lives of new Christians when they first encounter the reality of unredeemed humanity within the church. The story of conversion is often one of an initial experience like falling in love. There is a euphoria that accompanies the first dawning of an understanding of the love of God, the first realisation of the forgiveness of sins, the first experience of the power of the Holy Spirit. It can indeed seem as if all things are made new, both in ourselves and in our relationships with others.

Please God, this new-found love is also reflected in the welcome and acceptance that the new Christian finds in the fellowship of the church. God forbid that anyone should take this experience of wonder away from the new believer. But inevitably there comes a day of disillusionment.

It may come from a spiteful remark, made or overheard. It may come in a revelation of some wrong-doing in the life of another church member. It may be a betrayal of trust by a leader in the church. Not everything has been made new; some of the old is still there. Perhaps those initial experiences were all an illusion. It is a moment of crisis for the new believer.

In one sense disillusionment is a step forward: we are not supposed to live with illusions either about ourselves or about one another. Sooner or later we must face up to the fact of post-baptismal or post-conversion sin. There are three tenses to salvation: I *have been* saved from the penalty of sin; I *am being* saved from the power of sin; I *will be* saved from the presence of sin.

Here and now, I am only in the process of being saved from the power of sin, and that is true of my fellow believers too. Sin persists. 'If we claim to be without sin we deceive ourselves,' says the Apostle John, and he is talking to people within the church (1 John 1.8).

In the church we do not say that we have no sin, nor do we say that our fellow church-members have no sin, nor even that our church leaders have no sin. We have to recognise that sin persists in all of us. That does not excuse our sin, or give us permission to settle down to living in it. John goes on to say, 'No one who lives in Christ keeps on sinning. No one who continues in sin has either seen him or known him' (1 John 3.6).

We have to live with a divine discontent within ourselves about our own sinfulness, and we have to discover the divine remedy for living with the sinfulness of others, and the sooner after our conversion that we do this the better. The trick that we have to learn of living together in the fellowship of the church is forgiveness.

Forgiveness is much misunderstood. Forgiveness is not excusing sin or saying that it does not matter. It does matter, and it is not excusable, in the church or outside it. But stuff happens and we have to deal with it in a godly way, and the godly way is to forgive it.

Nor does forgiveness mean forgetting. It is impossible to suppose that, if we have suffered some serious trauma or wrong, something, say, that will affect us for the rest of our lives, that we shall ever forget it. Forgiveness is a matter of our attitude towards the person or persons who did us this wrong. It is not inevitable that we go through the rest of our lives nursing bitterness and resentment towards that person, or that we are estranged from them forever.

The first part of forgiveness is not to seek or take revenge. Our first instinct on being hit is to hit back. That is true of physical blows; it is true of unkind or accusing words; it is true of any sort of damage inflicted on our persons or property. The way of the world is to store up grievances and to perpetuate feuds, to inflict pain for pain and loss for loss.

All this, the Christian has to renounce. This is not an option in the Christian life; Jesus says over and over again, that if we want to be forgiven by God, that is to say that if we want to be spared the wrath of God, we must spare others our own wrath and forgive them. Many people caused Jesus to suffer, but Jesus never caused others to suffer in return, and that is the same attitude that we are to have in Christ Jesus.

This is not about our feelings, but about our words and deeds. My feelings may continue to be hurt, even deeply hurt, and forgiveness is not pretending that they are not. Forgiveness means not seeking to hurt the one who hurt me in return. This may be difficult in the heat of the moment, and it may go on being difficult as time goes by.

Jesus said that if someone strikes you on the right cheek, rather than striking him back in the heat of the moment, you should let him strike you again. That is instantaneous forgiveness. But there is an ongoing struggle as well: not to dwell on the scene, on the injustice that you have suffered, on the wickedness of your attacker and the punishment that he deserves, and how much you would like to see him get his own back.

There is a glib forgiveness that Christians sometimes employ: 'Of course I have forgiven him, but I am still not speaking to him.' That is not forgiveness at all; it is continuing to nurse the grudge, to let the offender feel the weight of our displeasure. Forgiveness means not to return offence with offence, wrath with wrath, or evil with evil.

The second step in forgiveness is to return evil with good. We are to take every opportunity to do good to those who have hurt us. The film *Invictus* tells the true story of how Nelson Mandela became the first President of South Africa under black-majority rule, and used his new position to bring reconciliation to the post-apartheid Republic.

Many white people feared that, now the blacks were in power, they would turn the tables and take revenge for the oppression that the black and coloured people had suffered under apartheid. On his first day in office, Mandela summoned the staff that he had inherited from his white predecessor. These white men and women expected to be sacked and replaced by black or coloured appointees more sympathetic to the new regime.

But Mandela gave them a fair choice: if they felt unable to serve their new president, he respected their right to resign and to leave, but if they wished to stay on in their posts, he would value their support and experience. This grace was extended even to the members of the Special Branch that had provided the former white, presidential bodyguard. They were invited to stay on and merge with Mandela's black ANC bodyguard.

There were tensions on both sides over this arrangement: Mandela's black bodyguards complaining that they were being expected to work with men who had only recently been beating up and even murdering their fellow blacks. 'Exactly,' replied Mandela, 'You represent an important principle. The Rainbow Nation starts here. Reconciliation starts here. Forgiveness starts here.'

This was not just an overlooking of wrongs done in general to his own race, grievous as those had been; Mandela himself had suffered twenty-seven years of harsh imprisonment on Robben Island as well as many personal humiliations and insults such as were suffered by all black and coloured people in apartheid South Africa. But

Mandela resisted the opportunity to take revenge on his former oppressors.

Forgiveness is more a matter of objective words and deeds than of feelings. In her book *Tramp for the Lord* Corrie ten Boom tells a story of preaching in a church in Munich in southern Germany in 1947. During the Second World War the Dutch ten Boom family had sheltered Jews in their house from Nazi persecution.

The family were betrayed and sent to concentration camps where Corrie's father and sister Betsie both died. After the war Corrie ten Boom spent many years before she died in 1983 preaching the need for forgiveness and reconciliation.

On one occasion while preaching in Munich, Corrie had recognised in the congregation the face of one of the most sadistic of the guards that she had known in the camp at Ravensbrück, a warder who had shamed and humiliated both her and her sister.

At the end of the service Corrie stood at the church door to greet the congregation as they left. With an overwhelming sense of dread she saw her former enemy approach with outstretched hand. The man spoke, 'You mentioned

Ravensbrück in your talk,' he said, 'I was a guard there. But since that time I have become a Christian. I know that God has forgiven me the cruel things that I did. Fraulein, will you forgive me too.'

'Jesus, help me, I do not know how to forgive this man,' Corrie prayed under her breath. In spite of this she stretched out her hand and took that of the man. It was as their hands made contact that her whole body was flooded with love and tenderness towards her former oppressor. 'I do forgive you, brother, with all my heart,' she cried.

It was the simple act of shaking hands that had released the feelings in her heart. Forgiveness is an act of faith and obedience, before it is a feeling. We make the mould of forgiveness with our wills and our words and our actions, and God fills the mould with his love.

All this is true of our relationships in the local church as much as on the stage of world affairs, and as much in the petty offences of everyday life as in the horrors of the concentration camp. And we must go on extending this forgiveness to those who hurt us not once or twice, but forever. Jesus said, not seven times, but seventy times seven or seventy-seven times: in other words, stop counting. The old English word for patience is *long-suffering*. It explains very well what is involved in living together, both in the church and the world.

No one has ever pretended that forgiveness is cheap. To see the cost of forgiveness we have only to look at the Cross: that is what it cost God to forgive us our sins, and our forgiveness of one another will be costly too.

As Jesus did, we have to experience the pain and the hurt, and, like a sponge, absorb it. We have to take it upon ourselves and let it stay with us, rather than trying to return it to the person from whom it came.

Nothing is gained by returning evil for evil: evil is only multiplied and perpetuated. The only way of dealing with evil is to absorb it, to bear it. That is the way of the Cross, and we are all called, as disciples of Jesus, to take up the Cross and follow him.

The apostle Paul very boldly calls this, 'filling up in my flesh what is still lacking in Christ's afflictions' (Colossians 1.24). He does not mean that there was anything more that God's Son needed to do to atone for the sins of the world, but that we are called, as members of Christ's body, to bear our share of those afflictions as we forgive those who sin against us.

Forgiveness is much easier when the offender, like Corrie ten Boom's persecutor, has already repented and apologised, but even that cannot be made a condition of our forgiveness. Jesus prayed for his persecutors, 'Father forgive them,' before there was any sign of repentance or remorse amongst them, and indeed there is no reason to suppose that there ever was.

Forgiveness is *fore*-giveness or *before*-giveness. Gordon Wilson, a local draper in Enniskillen in Northern Ireland and a devout Methodist, was buried in rubble in the bombing of the town by the Provisional IRA on Remembrance Day 1987. His daughter Marie, a nurse, was buried with him. Gordon survived; Marie did not.

In an interview with the BBC, Wilson described with anguish his last conversation with his daughter and his feelings toward her killers: 'She held my hand tightly, and gripped me as hard as she could. She said, "Daddy, I love you very much." Those were her exact words to me, and those were the last words I ever heard her say.'

Wilson then added, 'But I bear no ill will. I bear no grudge. Dirty sort of talk is not going to bring her back to life. She was a great wee lassie. She loved her profession. She was a pet. She's dead. She's in heaven and we shall meet again. I will pray for these men tonight and every night.'

Gordon Wilson went on to campaign for peace in Northern Ireland; he pleaded with the Loyalists not to take revenge; he went out of his way to meet with members of Sinn Fein and was appointed a member of the Senate by the Prime Minister of the Irish Republic.

All of this is primarily a matter of attitude. We may not have the means to take revenge even if we wanted to do so. We may not have the means to return evil with good. What is primarily required of us by God is an attitude: it is the opposite of the attitude of resentment and bitterness. It is an attitude in which the desire for vengeance is swallowed up by the desire for reconciliation and the restoration of relationships of friendship and harmony.

We want to be a blessing to our friends; Jesus challenges us to want to be a blessing to our enemies also. If the attitude is right, then when we do have the means to do good and to bless, then that attitude will find expression in words and deeds.

With all the good-will in the world we cannot prevent offenders from suffering the temporal consequences of their sin, nor the spiritual consequences unless they repent and turn to God. If a person has committed a crime, our forgiveness cannot and should not prevent the law from taking its course. If I have been mugged in the streets, I may be inclined to forgive my assailants, but I should not normally drop charges against them. Not only I, but other people, have the right to be protected against such attacks, and that is the function of the law.

There have been many recent scandals over the abuse of children by priests and pædophiles within the Roman Catholic Church. To forgive such abuse is included within the Christian requirement to forgive, hard though it may be, especially for the abused. But to ignore it or cover it up is not the same thing, and it is not a godly response. Everyone, including the authorities in the Church, now recognise that these matters should be brought to light and those guilty brought to justice. This is the only way for others to be protected from future abuse.

In the same way, indeed in an even more terrifying way, my forgiveness cannot take the place of the offender's own repentance and faith, if he or she is to escape the spiritual wages of sin and find peace with God. Paul sums the matter up in Romans 12.17-21:

> *Do not repay anyone evil for evil. Be careful to do what is right in the eyes of everybody. If it is possible, as far as it depends on you, live at peace with everyone. Do not take revenge, my friends, but leave room for God's wrath, for it is written: "It is mine to avenge; I will repay," says the Lord. On the contrary: "If your enemy is hungry, feed him; if he is thirsty, give him something to drink. In doing so, you will heap burning coals on his head." Do not be overcome by evil, but overcome evil with good.*

There is no better example of forgiveness in Scripture than the life of Joseph (Genesis 37-50). At the age of seventeen, Joseph was sold by his brothers to slave-traders and became a slave in Egypt. He was then falsely accused by his master's wife and put into prison.

After many vicissitudes, Joseph's life at length came to a place where the very members of his own family who had plotted against him and condemned him to suffering and misfortune, came into his power. His brothers came seeking corn in Egypt because there was a famine in the land of Canaan, and Joseph had the power to give it or withhold it, or to imprison his brothers as spies.

With the power to exact any revenge that he wanted, Joseph chose to bless his family, not only giving them the food that they needed but returning their payment for it, and eventually making provision, not only for his father but for all his brothers to settle in the best of the land of Egypt.

Even after the death of his father, Joseph's heart had no place for revenge towards his brothers. '"Don't be afraid," he said to them, "Am I in the place of God? You intended to harm me, but God intended it for good … So then, don't be afraid. I will provide for you and your children." And he reassured them and spoke kindly to them' (Genesis 50.19-21). May we reassure those who have hurt us and speak as kindly to them as Joseph did.

All this is true of all our relationships, in public life, in the family, in the work-place and in the neighbourhood. But we need to pay special attention to these things in our relationships in the church.

Paul recognised that it may not always be possible to live at peace with everyone. It takes two to make a quarrel, and it takes two to make it up. In the world, people are not always committed to making up their differences, and a wish to be reconciled may not be reciprocated. But in the fellowship of the church, this is something to which we should all be committed, and where we have a special responsibility to God to work it out together. How else can we be a light in the world?

The church should be a place, an unusual place, where a slight or a hurt does not lead to a permanent grudge or estrangement, where people know how to be reconciled and how to go on living together in peace and harmony.

To this end it is important to know the other members of the fellowship as more than just names or faces. In a large church this may be difficult, except in a small group, but the experience of getting to know a few people more closely can extend our sympathy to the others also.

A good exercise in a small Christian group is for each person to tell the story of their lives and of what God has done for them. A measure of trust is required if people are to open up and reveal their deepest hurts and pain, but even a superficial telling of someone's story will help the others to understand a little of what has made that person what he or she is.

Knowing is half way to loving. Pity is a much maligned virtue. 'I don't want your pity,' we say. Yes, you do. We all need each other's pity. We need God to have mercy on us, to pity us, and we need others to have mercy on us, to pity us too.

In one way or another all our lives are pitiful, and the more we are moved to pity, the less we shall be moved to condemn and the more we shall be moved to forgive. If we then also hear from a fellow Christian what God has already done in their lives, we shall realise that what is true of us is true of them: that we are all a work in progress, that God has not finished with any of us yet. We should therefore be patient with one another, not reinforcing that fear of rejection that torments our lives, but working with God in loving each other towards perfection.

Part of the forgiveness of the sins of others is not to gossip about them or spread disgraceful stories about them. It does no one any good to retell stories of the sins and shortcomings of others, whether we ourselves have been the victims or not. It benefits neither the teller nor the hearer nor the person about whom the story is told.

Paul points us in the opposite direction: 'Do not let any unwholesome talk come out of your mouths, but only what is helpful for building others up, according to their needs, that it may benefit those who listen' (Ephesians 4.29). Even in the Old Testament gossip was recognised to be a sin, 'You speak continually against your brother and slander your own mother's son' (Psalm 50.20).

The New Testament is even more forthright. James warns us of the damage that can be done by the tongue: 'Consider what a great forest can be set on fire by a small spark. The tongue also is a fire … With the tongue we praise our Lord and Father, and with it we curse men … My brothers this should not be,' (James 3.1-12).

How much trouble is stirred up in churches by the wagging of tongues! My mother used to say, 'If you can't find something nice to say about someone, don't say anything at all.'

So what do we do when someone in the church offends us, or when we see a fellow Christian falling into deliberate and persistent sin? What we do must depend on the seriousness of the sin and of the situation that it has caused.

Trivial things are best overlooked and forgiven without any more ado, in the church as in married life. But in a more serious matter, forgiveness does not mean that we simply ignore it, as if nothing had happened or as if nothing were going on? In such cases Jesus gives us a godly procedure to follow that is aimed at minimising the damage that sin does in the church to everyone concerned. The procedure is found in Matthew 18.15-18:

> *'If your brother sins against you, go and show him his fault, just between the two of you. If he listens to you, you have won your brother over. But if he will not*

> *listen, take one or two others along, so that "every matter may be established by the testimony of two or three witnesses". If he refuses to listen to them, tell it to the church: and if he refuses to listen even to the church, treat him as you would a pagan or a tax-collector. I tell you whatever you bind on earth will be bound in heaven, and whatever you loose on earth will be loosed in heaven.'*

The first thing to notice in these verses is that there is a textual uncertainty at the beginning: some manuscripts say, 'sin against you,' others simply say, 'sin.' The best policy is to assume that Jesus meant both: whether the sin affects you personally or not, this is the procedure to follow.

First, go and talk to your Christian brother or sister privately; 'show him his fault' (verse 15). If this advice were always followed we would already have saved a great deal of trouble in the church.

Unfortunately, too often the first reaction of people is the opposite: either to go and complain to the pastor or vicar, or to tell everyone else in the church except the offender what the offender has done and what we think of them. If someone in the church has hurt you, first complain *to them.* Or if you have direct, first-hand knowledge that a fellow Christian is behaving in an ungodly way, then confront them yourself.

All this presupposes, I repeat, that the matter is sufficiently serious to be taken up in such a way at all. God forbid that we should go around continually finding fault with one another, or nit-picking about one another's behaviour; there would be no end to it.

Some sins however are more serious. Sins are like diseases: some diseases get better of their own accord, while others only get worse and spread if they are left untreated. It needs a measure of discrimination to know when to speak up and when to keep silent. Sometimes at least, we need to go and 'show our brother his sin.'

Jesus goes on, 'If your brother listens to you, you have won your brother over' (verse 15). But if he will not listen, then take one or two other discrete and sensible people along with you and go over it again. The others are there to act as referees or mediators or witnesses, to help you to resolve your differences, or to reinforce your warning.

If all else fails then involve the leadership of the church, with whom will lie the ultimate responsibility of resolving the matter. But the aim of the whole process is to bring an offender to repentance, and to bring estranged members of the church together in peace and reconciliation. The hope of such conversations is the restoration of fellowship and forgiveness.

Paul says again:

> *Therefore, as God's chosen people, holy and dearly loved, clothe yourselves with compassion, kindness, humility, gentleness and patience. Bear with each other and forgive whatever grievances you may have against one another. Forgive as the Lord forgave you. And over all these virtues put on love that binds them all together in perfect unity* (Colossians 3.12-14).

Of course, we have to remember that any of us may be the offender rather than the offended. Our care for the unity of the fellowship of the church must extend, not only to how we react to those who offend us, but also to how we handle the situations in which we ourselves have offended other people. Our offence may be directly against a fellow believer in the church, or we may offend them and God by living disorderly or dishonest lives in the world outside.

A Christian who is often heard cursing and swearing and using profane language can offend others believers whether the remarks are made about them or about some other subject altogether. We may hope to be rebuked and corrected by Christian friends, but we cannot escape the responsibility of monitoring our own conduct as it appears in the eyes of God and in the eyes of others.

There was a lot to be said for the old, Catholic, practice of sacramental confession. It involved believers examining themselves and confessing their sins to another Christian, the priest, and seeking from him godly advice as well as absolution, and some act of penance or restitution.

Today we might call it accountability, and perhaps a more acceptable way today for many Christians to practice such accountability is to select a fellow believer and ask to be accountable to them. In terms of more mature Christians this can be a relationship of mutual accountability.

A new Christian, on the other hand, should rather seek out a more mature believer to act as a mentor. It should always be someone of the same sex. From time to time some churches have tried to practice this sort of accountability and confession either before the whole congregation or in small groups.

Such experiments have usually failed, through the indiscretion of other members of the group and the irresistible temptation to gossip. But some such commitment to complete openness with a fellow believer is a worthwhile and powerful discipline in the Christian life.

Whether we decide to make ourselves accountable to someone else or not, we all need to take responsibility for our own conduct and behaviour, not least towards our fellow Christians in the church. That means examining all our relationships from time to time and putting right any wrongs that we may have done towards others as quickly and completely as possible. Such self-examination can be a part of our prayers at the end of each day.

Before we go to church to receive the Holy Communion is another important time to review our relationships, with God and with other people in the church. Paul tells us, 'A man ought to examine himself before he eats of the bread or drinks of the cup' (1 Corinthians 11.28). The Anglican Book of Common Prayer also contains much godly wisdom on this subject, even if it is couched in somewhat quaint language:

> *First, examine your lives and conversations by the rule of God's commandments; and wherein ye shall perceive yourselves to have offended, either by will, word, or deed, there to bewail your own sinfulness, and to confess yourselves to Almighty God, with full purpose of amendment of life. And if ye shall perceive your offences to be such as are not only against God, but also against your neighbours; then ye shall reconcile yourselves unto them; being ready to make restitution and satisfaction, according to the uttermost of your powers, for all injuries and wrongs done by you to any other; and being likewise ready to forgive others that have offended you, as you would have forgiveness of your offences at God's hand.*

There are several elements in this process. The first is self-examination: some sort of systematic review of our lives, our relationships and our conduct. The Ten Commandments provide a useful starting point to quicken our consciences and remind us of the different areas of our lives that we need to consider. The second step is confession: certainly confession before God, but maybe also confession to a discrete and trusted friend in the Lord. There is great power in receiving the assurance of God's forgiveness from someone who has heard and knows the worst about us, with them using perhaps the words of 1 John 1.5-9:

> *This is the message we have heard from him and declare to you: God is light; in him there is no darkness at all. If we claim to have fellowship with him yet walk in darkness, we lie and do not live by the truth. But if we walk in the light, as he is in the light, we have fellowship with one another, and the blood of Jesus, his Son, purifies us from all sin. If we claim to be without sin, we deceive ourselves and the truth is not in us. If we*

> *confess our sins, he is faithful and just and will forgive us our sins and purify us from all unrighteousness.*

The third step is restitution: apologising where necessary, and making whatever amends we can for the wrong we have done. It is amazing how much is achieved by the simple words, 'I'm sorry.'

Fourthly, we have to resolve to amend our lives in the future, not to repeat the sin or the wrong. Amendment of life can take a long time, and may involve seeking the help and prayer and counsel of others. Some habits and bondages may have a demonic root and need to be dealt with accordingly. Others may have roots in emotional and psychological traumas that also need to be exposed to the light and healed.

None of us should be too proud to admit our inability to overcome a persistent or besetting sin, and to seek the help of godly and loving friends. Lastly, we have to be committed to forgiving others, as we hope and trust that God and others will forgive us, which is where, in this chapter, we came in.

When we have examined all the ways in which our friendships and fellowship in the church can break down, perhaps we are in a good place to hear what Paul has to say about the nature and quality of love for one another:

> *'Love is patient, love is kind. It does not envy, it does not boast, it is not proud. It is not rude, it is not self-seeking, it is not easily angered, it keeps no record of wrongs. Love does not delight in evil, but rejoices in the truth. It always protects, always trusts, always hopes, always perseveres.'* (1 Corinthians 13.4-7)

Chapter Eight

KEEPING THE UNITY OF THE SPIRIT: 2

There are other issues that break the unity of the Spirit in the fellowship of the church: doctrinal ones. Already, in Apostolic times, such causes of division were threatening the integrity of the early church.

When Paul took leave of the elders of Ephesus he warned them that, 'Even from your own number men will arise and distort the truth in order to draw away disciples after them' (Acts 20.30). John also warns, 'If anyone comes to you and does not bring this teaching (that Jesus Christ has come in the flesh), do not take him into your house or welcome him' (2 John 10).

History is littered with the heresies and schisms that have divided the church and many differences of doctrine have become institutionalised in the denominations and sects that surround us today. From the early disputes about the divinity of Christ and the nature of the Trinity, through the Great Schism between East and West in the Middle Ages, to the doctrinal ferment of the Reformation, the history of the church is one of zealous and often fierce contention between the protagonists of rival teachings.

It has not been edifying, but perhaps it was inevitable. Paul says again, 'I hear that there are divisions among you and to some extent I believe it. No doubt there have to be divisions among you to show which of you have God's approval' (1 Corinthians 11.18-19).

Perhaps what has been unedifying in so many church divisions, up to today, is not so much the differences in doctrine themselves, but the manner in which these differences and the subsequent divisions have been handled. If we have to disagree, and Paul suggests that sometimes we do in order for the truth to become plain, then we should disagree graciously and with some generosity of spirit, rather than bitterly and rancorously, and even violently, as so often in the past.

There is a model in the life of Paul himself, a disagreement not over doctrine but over a matter of personal judgement, but nevertheless a model of how to handle disagreements amongst believers in a way that does not disgrace the gospel.

Paul and Barnabas agreed to set out to revisit the churches that they had planted on their first missionary journey (Acts 15.36-41). They disagreed about the wisdom of taking with them John Mark. Since there was no way of resolving this disagreement, they decided to part company and go their separate ways, Barnabas taking Mark, and Paul Silas.

It was an amicable way to settle the matter, and a positive way because it resulted in two teams going out instead of one. The quarrel did not lead to a lasting estrangement, for later, we hear Paul speaking warmly again of Mark (2 Timothy 4.11). Separation between believers is less than ideal, but a gracious and amicable separation is less damaging to the Kingdom of God than a long drawn out battle, whether of swords or words or court cases.

Nevertheless, we do have to ask ourselves whether all our doctrinal differences require separation or whether there are not ways in which we can live together and agree to differ. There are clearly issues that are so fundamental that we cannot embrace differing views without compromising the truth of the gospel. I believe that those early disputes about the person of Christ and the nature of the Trinity were of this sort.

The formation of the canon of Scripture in the first three centuries can be seen as the Church defining the boundaries of orthodox doctrine. The purpose of this fixing of the boundaries is clearly set out in the Anglican Articles of Religion, in a way that expresses not just the mind of the Anglican Church in the 17th century, but the mind of the universal church in establishing the canon: 'Holy Scripture containeth all things necessary to salvation: so that whatsoever is not read therein, nor may be proved thereby, is not to be required of any man, that it should be believed as an article of Faith, or be thought requisite or necessary to salvation' (Article VI, Book of Common Prayer).

There is both a positive and a negative statement in this Article: positively, the Scriptures do contain everything that we need to know and believe for our salvation; negatively, we should not fall out over matters that are not clearly taught in them.

Since the establishment of the canon, divergences of doctrine within the church have revolved around the interpretation of Scripture. Personally, I have developed a rule of thumb over the years that says, 'If it is necessary to our salvation it is clear in scripture; if it is not clear then it is not necessary.' I would go on to add that if it is not clear in Scripture and not essential to our salvation, then I believe that we should try to find ways of living together with our doctrinal differences rather than separating over inessentials.

Underlying this, there is in fact a Scriptural principle and precedent. It is clear that in the earliest, apostolic churches there were doctrinal differences, great and small, and that Paul himself strove to separate the greater from the smaller, and to deal with them in different ways.

The great controversy was over circumcision. Once the gospel had been preached to the Gentiles, the question arose whether Gentile converts had to become Jews, to be circumcised and accept the full weight of the law of Moses, before they could become Christians, believe in the Jewish Messiah and become members of the household of God. This was a point on which for Paul, and ultimately the whole church, there could be no compromise.

For Paul the teaching of the Judaizers constituted 'a different gospel' (Galatians 1.6). On the other hand, there arose many disputes over the eating of different foods and the keeping of different holy days.

None of these seemed to Paul to be of the essence of the gospel and could therefore be accommodated within the fellowship of the church with tolerance and understanding (Romans 14). The trick has been, and still is, to distinguish the one sort of dispute from the other.

I guess that I have always been influenced by the church in which I grew up, the Hampstead Garden Suburb Free Church in London. When the Hampstead Garden Suburb was being built in the early years of the 20th century, land was allocated for two churches: one for a parish church for the Anglicans, the other a plot for the Non-conformist or Free Churches.

The second of these churches was founded in 1910 by a group of people, including my own grandfather, drawn from several different denominations, who agreed to work and to worship together, and to build a church that would be a sign of their fundamental unity in Christ.

In its time this was a remarkable initiative. The church became affiliated to the Baptist Union, the Congregational Union and the Presbyterian Church of England. Of my own four grandparents who lived on the Suburb, one was an Anglican, a choir-man at St Paul's Cathedral, the other three were all members of the Free Church, a Baptist, a Methodist and a Presbyterian.

On the walls of this church are inscribed the words of the ancient formulary sometimes attributed to St Augustine, 'In things necessary, unity; in things doubtful, liberty; in all thing, charity.' It worked, and I have tried to maintain that ideal all my life. But the trick is to distinguish the necessary from the doubtful.

There were two great movements in Christianity in the 20th century: the Ecumenical Movement and the Charismatic or Pentecostal Movement. The first sought the reunion of the historic churches, the second breathed new life into them. The first of these largely failed in its aim of securing institutional reunion between the churches and petered out in a series of interminable committees and conversations most of which led nowhere.

But the process was not without fruit: relationships between the historic denominations changed from their former antagonism and hostility to a new tolerance and respect. Local churches now meet together and work together on common projects of witness and service, and, in an increasingly indifferent or even hostile culture, we are more likely to feel that Christians of other denominations are our friends rather than our enemies.

The very exercise of meeting together with members of other churches, whether for theological conversations or for cooperation on more practical projects, has bred a new love and respect for one another that is probably more important in the eyes of God than ponderous schemes for institutional reunion.

However, at the same time as the Ecumenical Movement has brought Christians together across the historic divides, the Pentecostal and Charismatic Movements have introduced new divisions into the Christian scene. New denominations and new churches sprang up where the renewal of the gifts of the Holy Spirit caused division in the older churches.

Paradoxically, the result of these two movements in the 20th century has been that there are now likely to be more churches and congregations in town than there used to be, but at the same time that there is less friction and more cooperation between them.

Indeed, amongst the charismatic churches at least, there is now an extraordinary convergence of forms and orders of worship and ministry, and an indifference amongst Christians, especially younger Christians, to narrow denominational and doctrinal allegiances. A person today, especially a young person, is more likely to identify themselves as a Christian or a non-Christian, and less likely to identify themselves as an Anglican or a Methodist, a Baptist or a Pentecostal.

Doctrinal differences however do remain, and indeed new ones have sprung up that tend to cause division and separation. So the question of how we handle these differences has not gone away. By way of example, we shall look at three of these issues and the lessons that can be learned from them.

Since the 16th century, baptism has been a source of controversy among the churches: some churches believe in and practice infant baptism, others insist that before baptism a person must profess the faith for themselves. I personally am persuaded, on both Scriptural and historical grounds, that the Church has baptised the children of believing parents ever since the Day of Pentecost (Acts 2.39).

However, I recognise that others, equally sincerely, take a different view. Another aspect of this controversy surrounds the method of baptism: by immersion or aspersion. These controversies have gone on now for over 500 years without either side being able to convince the other, and perhaps we all need to admit that our arguments, both Scriptural and historical, are less than conclusive.

Can we then not find a way of living together with these disagreements while maintaining the unity of the Spirit in the bond of peace? It is not too difficult, provided that we do not insist on forcing our persuasions upon others.

In the Fountain of Life Church, for which I was responsible in Norfolk, we gave to parents the responsibility of deciding whether to have their infants baptised or not, and if so how. I have always been happy to baptise the babies of believing parents, and if parents declared their own faith and intention of bringing their children up in the fellowship of the church, then I gladly baptised their offspring.

I have baptised babies by both immersion and aspersion, as the parents requested. If, on the other hand, parents decided to leave their children to make up their own minds about baptism later in life, I was happy to honour that decision, and their children have grown up in the fellowship of the church until they were willing and able to profess the faith for themselves.

The only difficulty with this regime occurs when a person who was baptised as an infant wants to express their adult commitment to Christ by being re-baptised, or, as they might see it, validly baptised for the first time. I found the solution in an article by Michael Green, drawing on the experience of Roman Catholic and other churches in South America. Such an adult enters the baptismal pool and the minister says, 'N or

M, you were baptised as an infant at the request of your parents, now, on the profession of your own faith and at your own request, we re-enact your baptism, in the Name of the Father, and of the Son, and of the Holy Spirit.' The candidate is then immersed in the water. This formula seems to satisfy and honour everyone, and has proved a way of holding together in the same fellowship those who hold different views on this divisive issue.

The second issue that we shall explore here is that of Christian Zionism and different doctrines of the End Times. These are comparatively modern controversies often entangled with political implications, whether about affairs in the Middle East or about climate change.

There are those who believe that the foundation of the State of Israel in 1948 was the fulfilment of Old Testament prophecy and that it is a fundamental part of God's plan that Israel should recover the land promised to Abraham, Isaac and Jacob before the End comes. Others, and this is the traditional teaching of all the churches, believe that those who believe in Jesus are the true Israel, rather than the descendants of Abraham according to the flesh, and that the promises of the Old Testament are to be interpreted in the light of the New Testament Kingdom of God.

This dispute is often compounded with disputes about the interpretation of the millennium, described in Revelation 20. There are a variety of scenarios anticipating the End Times: pre-millennialism, post-millennialism, and a-millennialism. Passions often run so high over these doctrines that they split churches. Can we maintain the unity of the Spirit in the bond of peace in the face of these differences? Again, I believe that we can, provided that we do not insist in imposing our views on others.

It can hardly be maintained that the doctrine of the millennium is clear in Scripture. The rest of the New Testament, including the teaching of Jesus in the Gospels, makes no mention of a millennium: we simply await the return of the Lord Jesus, the Last Judgement, the new heaven and the new earth (Matthew 24-25, Mark 13, Luke 17.20-37, 21.5-36, 1 Corinthians 15.12-58, 1 Thessalonians 4.13-5.11, 2 Thessalonians 2.1-12, 2 Peter 3).

Jesus prophesied the dispersion of the Jews and the desolation of Jerusalem, but nowhere does the New Testament say anything about the return of the Jews to the Promised Land. If the Scriptures contain all things necessary for our salvation, it is difficult to insist that any of these obscure and controversial teachings about the End Times are to be regarded as issues over which we should divide the church.

The Orthodox Churches of the East have always maintained a distinction between articles of faith and pious opinions. If questions of the End Times and the State of Israel are accepted as pious opinions rather than as articles of faith, then we can press on together with the more immediate task that Jesus has set before us: preaching the Kingdom and doing the works that he did wherever we live.

After all, we do not need to know now what will happen when the Lord comes again in order to tell the story of what Jesus has done for us and for our salvation, and to be fellow-workers with him for the Kingdom of God.

While the apostles stood still, gazing up into heaven, watching Jesus go, the angel rebuked them (Acts 1.11). They had their commission: this was not to worry about times or dates that the Father had fixed by his own authority, nor to worry about his restoring the kingdom to Israel; their commission was to be witnesses to Jesus in Jerusalem, in Judea and Samaria, and to the ends of the earth (Acts 1.6-8).

The remedy for quarrelling about the End Times or the State of Israel is for the church to focus on the Great Commission and avoid foolish controversies that are unprofitable and useless (Titus 3.9). There is quite enough for any Christian or church to do in making disciples, baptising them, and teaching them to obey everything that Jesus has commanded, to keep us all busy until he surprises us by coming again. We are too good at letting disputes over ever more arcane and unnecessary points of doctrine distract us from building the Kingdom of God.

The third issue that has arisen in recent years to disturb the unity of the church is homosexuality. In Western societies in the last fifty years there has been a revolution in the way in which homosexuality is regarded and treated by the law. This change has been driven by aggressive campaigning in politics and the media to promote a view of homosexuality that is contrary to both Scripture and to natural law.

These campaigns have influenced many inside as well as outside the churches, and only those who maintain a strong doctrine of revelation in the Scriptures and a firm hold on common sense have stood out against this tide of popular opinion.

This issue seems to me to be one on which there can be no alternative to separation. A church that believes that homosexual practice is a perversion of the purposes of God in creation must confront and discipline those who adopt a homosexual way of life. There is no way of combining such discipline with another practice that welcomes and blesses those who are living in a homosexual relationship.

'In things necessary, unity; in things doubtful, liberty; in all things, charity.' We have to decide which things are necessary and which are doubtful.

As I have explained above, I would consider the age and method of baptism as things doubtful, the interpretation of Old Testament prophecy about the people of Israel and of New Testament prophecy about the millennium as things doubtful, but I would consider the question of the Scriptural doctrine of sexuality as beyond doubt and therefore as something necessary to our salvation. We need to consider long and hard which things come into which category, but when we have considered them, then we must accept that the only way forward in the face of fundamental disagreement, is separation, however difficult and painful that may be.

Within the life of my own denomination, the Church of England and the worldwide Anglican Communion, such a separation raises major issues. Can one local church within the denomination, or even one diocese or province, maintain one doctrine and discipline over homosexuality, and a neighbouring church another?

Such a basic inconsistency seems impossible to accommodate. Already in North America there are *de facto* two Anglican denominations, and it is difficult to see how this split cannot spread through the whole Communion, and even through the Church of England. The idea of separation is not congenial to a church that prides itself on being 'broad.' But unless the gospel is to be emptied of all content, there must be limits to the breadth of doctrine and practice that a church can embrace.

Issues of doctrine, and the consequent issues of practice that follow in the case of matters such as those connected with human sexuality, are issues that cause division in the fellowship of the church as much as personal issues.

We have looked at three such doctrinal issues and the ways in which they can be handled. Some of them can be accommodated within the fellowship, provided that people, including the leaders, do not insist in imposing their opinions on others in matters that are unclear or inessential to the gospel of salvation. But other issues arise in which there is no way forward except to separate from one another.

This is not necessarily the worst outcome, provided that the separation is not accompanied by disgraceful exhibitions of backbiting and internecine fighting. Let God be the judge. As Gamaliel advised, 'Let them go! For if their purpose or activity is of human origin, it will fail. But if it is from God you will not be able to stop these men; you will only find yourselves fighting against God' (Acts 5.38-39).

The perfect unity of the people of God belongs to the new heavens and the new earth, not to this one. Here, we have to live with causes of division and to handle them with as much grace as we can.

Chapter Nine

THE IDEA OF INCLUSIVITY

We have noticed in several previous chapters that there are occasions when people have to be excluded from the fellowship of believers or when the fellowship has to be split. This is a difficult idea, and an even more difficult process, for most of us to contemplate, and for some Christians both the idea and the process are simply unacceptable.

Western culture is allergic to the idea of exclusion on any grounds. Our laws and regulations are designed to prevent discrimination on the grounds of race, religion, class, wealth, gender, or sexual preference. Our recognition of Human Rights and the freedom of individual choice mean that it is not politically correct to question anyone's beliefs or lifestyle or to make these the grounds for any sort of social exclusion.

'Exclusion' has become a political boo-word, while 'inclusion' has become a political 'hurrah-word'. In the controversy in the Episcopal Church in the USA over the ordination of homosexuals and the blessing of homosexual relationships, great play has been made of the church's 'inclusivity.' One such congregation advertises itself as follows:

> *The Church of the Redeemer in Morristown, one of New Jersey's most welcoming and accepting churches. The sign on our front lawn says it all, "We Are One Family". All are welcome to visit and worship with us. In the spirit of diversity and* ***inclusivity****, we invite you to visit us if you are: male, female, white, black, senior, child, gay, straight, infant, liberal, a dreamer, Christian, non-Christian, questioning, partnered, single, transgendered, in recovery, searching, young, conservative, or a nun.* (emphasis my own)

The church describes itself as 'a come-as-you-are party'. It would be anathema to this church to exclude anyone on the grounds of either their beliefs or their lifestyle.

Beyond this, however, many other, more orthodox, Christians have reasons to find the practice of excluding people from the fellowship of the church unacceptable. Jesus, they argue, went out of his way to welcome those who were excluded from respectable, God-fearing, society.

He was notorious as 'a friend of tax-collectors and sinners'. He kept company with gluttons and drunkards and was not afraid to be tarred with the same brush (Matthew 11.19). He accepted the love of a woman of the streets, defending her against Simon the Pharisee (Luke 7.36-50). His willingness to mix with the outcasts and morally despised, and his unwillingness to condemn them, caused scandal and alarm, offence and opposition, amongst the righteous and respectable. It was the scribes and Pharisees who excluded sinners; Jesus was inclusive.

All this is true as far as it goes, but it does not go far enough. When the woman who had been caught in the act of adultery was brought to Jesus, it is true that he did not condemn her, but neither did he condone what she had done or give her permission to go on committing adultery. His last words to her were, 'Go now, and leave your life of sin' (John 8.11).

There is a third alternative to condemnation or condonation: the call to repentance and holiness. There is a condition to entering the Kingdom of God: it is not sinlessness, but it is repentance. The preaching of both Jesus and John the Baptist begins with the words, 'Repent, for the Kingdom of heaven is at hand' (Matthew 3.2, 4.17).

This introduces a tension into the life of the Kingdom that we have already remarked: the tension between the persistence of the life of the old nature, alongside the new life of the Spirit within us. It is Paul who most clearly analyses this tension (e.g. Galatians 5). 'It is for freedom that Christ has set us free,' he begins (verse 1). But this freedom is not freedom *to* sin but freedom *from* sin. Sin is a form of slavery, from which Christ has redeemed us, and into which it is foolishness for us to fall back. 'Stand firm then,' Paul continues, 'and do not let yourselves be burdened again by a yoke of slavery.'

The difficulty we have with this doctrine is that we have long been deceived by Satan into thinking that sin is fun, that to set sin aside is to be a kill-joy. According to this understanding, which goes back to the Garden of Eden, God is the original spoil-sport, only intent on stopping us from having a good time. But nothing could be further from the truth. Sin is sin specifically because it has evil consequences, both for ourselves and for others. The definition of sin could be: those behaviours that have evil consequences for us and for others.

In *The Poisonwood Bible* the novelist Barbara Kingsolver writes, 'God does not have to punish us. He just lets us live long enough to punish ourselves.'

If we take the perspective of eternity into account, that tells us all we need to know about the justice of God and the nature of sin. If we finally reject God, then we shall spend eternity shut out from the presence of God, by our own choice. If we persist in sin we shall reap the harvest of sin, which is death and destruction.

We do not do anyone a favour by condoning their sin. Love must mean doing all that we can to dissuade each other and to help each other to depart from sinful acts and habits. So Paul goes on, 'You were called to be free. But do not use your freedom to indulge the sinful nature; rather serve one another in love' (Galatians 5.13).

This understanding of the Christian life underlies Jesus' own prescription for dealing with sin in the fellowship of believers, at which we looked in a previous chapter: Matthew 18.15-17.

This is a recipe for a loving watching over one another lest we fall back into that very slavery from which Christ has set us free. It is not an easy thing to do in practice; we can either become sanctimonious and censorious on the one hand, or careless and indifferent on the other. But we have to try, for everyone's sake, including the Lord's sake.

The ultimate sanction that Jesus imposes on an unrepentant sinner is that the church should 'treat him as you would a pagan or a tax-collector' (verse 17). This is the same Jesus who welcomed sinners and ate with tax-collectors, who called a tax-collector to be one of the Twelve, but who will not condone gross and persistent sin in the church.

We see Paul himself following this same discipline and practice in the church in Corinth (1 Corinthians 5). This passage illustrates all the questions that church discipline raises. It concerns a case of sexual immorality (verse 1). Sexual immorality so often seems to be the issue, but Paul makes it clear that it is not the only issue about which we should be concerned in our common life together: the same considerations apply to someone who is 'greedy, an idolater, a slanderer, a drunkard or a swindler' (verse 11).

Paul expected the believers in Corinth themselves to have dealt appropriately with the sexually immoral man (verse 2). It is only because they have not done so that Paul intervenes and tells them what they should do. The sanction that is to be applied to this sexually immoral man is exclusion from the church's gatherings and common meals, including, as those common meals did, the Lord's Supper (verse 13). This is the same sanction as Jesus prescribed, 'treat him as you would a pagan or a tax-collector.'

The purposes of this discipline are clear. They are twofold: first, the fellowship is to be protected from the contagion of sin; like yeast in a lump of dough, the corruption of sin can quickly spread through the entire fellowship. But second, it is for the ultimate benefit of the sinner himself.

What Paul means exactly by, 'hand this man over to Satan, so that the sinful nature may be destroyed and his spirit saved on the day of the Lord,' I am not sure. But it is clear that in the end the sanction is supposed to be remedial.

Paul also makes it clear that there are different rules for associating with sinful and immoral people inside and outside the church:

> *I have written to you in my letter not to associate with sexually immoral people – not at all meaning the people of this world who are immoral, or the greedy and swindlers, or idolaters. In that case you would have to leave the world. But now I am writing to you that you must not associate with anyone who calls himself a brother but is sexually immoral or greedy.* (1 Corinthians 5.9-11)

We have, as Christians, a dual calling: to love one another as fellow believers, and to love the unsaved who are still 'in the world.' It is not easy to fulfil both callings at once.

We see the tension illustrated in two kinds of church today: there are churches like the Exclusive Brethren who take the commandment to 'Come out from among them,' so seriously that their members have minimal contact with anyone outside their own fellowship. Exclusive Brethren could never be accused of eating with tax-collectors and sinners; they do not even eat with fellow Christians.

At the other extreme are churches like the Church of the Redeemer in Morristown New Jersey - churches that are so liberal in their 'inclusivity' that there is no difference between the beliefs and lifestyles of the worshippers and the beliefs and lifestyles of the society around them. In the one case, the salt of the earth is kept safely stored up in the salt-cellar; in the other, the salt has lost its savour altogether.

A balanced New Testament view of the matter is that the followers of Jesus are to be like him, freely associating with the moral outcasts of society (and equally with those who are merely conformed to the general immorality of society), but that becoming a follower of Jesus means a radical transformation of our way of life, a re-birth into a new way of life in which the old ways, the socially acceptable as well as the socially unacceptable, are left behind.

Paul continued his admonitions to the believers in Corinth: 'Do not be deceived: neither the sexually immoral nor idolaters nor adulterers nor male prostitutes nor homosexual offenders nor thieves nor the greedy nor drunkards nor slanderers, nor swindlers will inherit the kingdom of God. And that is what some of you were. But you were washed, you were sanctified, you were justified in the name of the Lord Jesus Christ and by the Spirit of God' (1 Corinthians 6.9-11).

There is a clear distinction between what these believers *were,* and what they now *are.* Becoming a Christian has changed them and required them to change. There is no continuing in or going back to the old ways.

The idea and practice of church discipline continued long after the Apostolic era. We saw Tertullian around 200 AD claiming that, 'with a great gravity is the work of judging carried on among us, as befits those who feel assured that they are in the sight of God; and you have the most notable example of judgment to come when any one has sinned so grievously as to require his severance from us in prayer, in the congregation and in all sacred intercourse.'

In the centuries of Catholic Christendom and in the State churches of the Reformation these disciplines fell largely into disuse, except as instruments of political manipulation. But fresh moves of the Spirit of God and fresh revivals of church life have always involved a rediscovery of the importance of the practice of a loving watchfulness and discipline over one another's lives. At the Reformation the Church of England tried to revive a godly discipline amongst its members, despite continuing to be a national church. The Book of Common Prayer provides wise and compassionate guidance for those with the responsibility of exercising such discipline.

> *If any be an open and notorious evil liver, or have done any wrong to his neighbours by word or deed, so that the congregation be thereby offended; the Curate* (person with the cure of souls*), having knowledge thereof, shall call him and advertise him, that in any wise he presume not to come to the Lord's Table, until he have openly declared himself to have truly repented and amended his former naughty life, that the congregation may thereby be satisfied which before were offended.* (Rubric to the service of Holy Communion)

There is much godly wisdom and important safeguards built into this procedure. First, the offence must be 'open and notorious.' In the case of sexual deviations, the fact that two men or two women share the same house should not automatically be assumed to indicate a homosexual relationship.

One of the sad consequences of the flaunting of homosexual relationships today is that the idea of simple friendship and companionship between people of the same sex has become discredited. In my own childhood, households of two or three middle-aged women were commonplace. These women were the girls whose potential husbands had been killed in the First World War, leaving them a generation of single women.

Since it is not good for the man or the woman to live alone, many of these women lived together, without any suspicion that their relationships were sexual. Perhaps sometimes they were; but if so, they were discrete and hidden. That of course would not justify them, but we are not called upon to go around poking our noses into the lives, and especially the bedrooms, of other people.

Only if there is '*open and notorious* evil living' is it necessary for pastors to intervene. Otherwise the nature of the relationship should remain a matter between the parties involved and their God.

The purpose of pastoral intervention, when it is necessary, is two-fold. The first is that 'the congregation be not thereby offended.' This does not only mean that the congregation should not be scandalised, but also that the offence should not spread throughout the congregation. This was one cause of Paul's concern when he insisted on the discipline of the immoral man in Corinth, that he should be expelled from the congregation: 'Don't you know that a little yeast works through the whole batch of dough?' (1 Corinthians 5.1-13).

All forms of sexual immorality, fornication and adultery as well as homosexuality, if left unchecked, will spread like a plague through a congregation, as they have done through society at large. It is for the protection and strengthening of others in the fellowship that 'open and notorious evil living' has to be confronted.

The second purpose of discipline in the church is to bring the offender to repentance and amendment of life. If the same case is in view in 2 Corinthians 2.5-11 as in 1 Corinthians 6, as many people think it is, then the discipline of the immoral man in Corinth would seem to have had the desired result. Paul's exhortation now is to receive the offender back into the fellowship of the church with comfort and forgiveness.

As the pastor of a church myself, I had on several occasions to confront and warn people who were openly adopting a lifestyle inconsistent with the Scriptures. To expel a believer from the fellowship of the church and to refuse to give them Holy Communion is to wield a very big spiritual stick. In an age in which most of the population have voluntarily excommunicated themselves, simply by absenting themselves from worship, it might seem a trivial sanction. But to someone who values their relationship with Jesus and his followers, it is a very severe punishment.

In some instances in my own experience, the shock has been sufficient to bring the offender to his or her senses and to lead to repentance and readmission into the fellowship of the church. In other cases, the result has been less satisfactory. But that is in the hands of God.

The Methodist movement in the 18th and 19th centuries was another revival that also involved the revival of church discipline. The strength of early Methodism lay in the societies, classes and bands into which the converts were gathered.

John Wesley was a great revivalist preacher, but the lasting success of his preaching relied not only on the initial response of his hearers to the message of salvation, but even more on the organization that Wesley established to nurture his converts. He looked in vain to the established churches to provide the care that his new Christians needed:

> *'Who watched over them in love? Who marked their growth in grace? Who advised and exhorted them from time to time? Who prayed with them and for them as they had need? This and this alone is Christian fellowship. But alas! where is it to be found? Look east or west, north or south; name what parish you please: is there Christian fellowship there? Rather, are not the bulk of the parishioners a mere rope of sand? What Christian connexion is there between*

> *them? What intercourse in spiritual things? What watching over each other's souls? What bearing of one another's burdens?'* (John Wesley, *A Plain Account of the People Called Methodists,* 1748)

It was this lack of real Christian fellowship that Wesley sought to remedy through his Methodist societies, classes and bands. Methodist societies, which in course of time became the local Methodist churches, were to be 'a company of men (Wesley had not the 21st century sensitivity about using gender-inclusive language) having the form and seeking the power of godliness, united in order to pray together, to receive the word of exhortation, and to watch over one another in love, that they may help each other to work out their own salvation.'

These aims of the Society were carried out in detail in the classes. Each class leader was responsible for meeting with each member once a week 'in order to enquire how their souls prosper; to advise, reprove, comfort, or exhort, as occasion may require.'

The role was essentially pastoral; through the class leader the preachers and leaders of the local society were kept informed of the needs of the sick and the poor. But the class was also the means of discipline: through the class system 'evil men were detected and reproved. They were born with for a season. If they forsook their sins, we received them gladly; if they obstinately persisted therein, it was openly declared that they were not of us. The rest mourned and prayed for them, and yet rejoiced, that, as far as in us lay, the scandal had been rolled away from the society.'

The band was an even smaller group within the Society, a gathering of just a few people of the same sex, who met together for mutual and open confession of their sins. The leader of each band was required to describe his own state first, and then 'to ask the rest, in order, as many and as searching questions as may be, concerning their state, sins and temptations.'

Nor did the Methodist leaders, from Wesley downwards, shrink from imposing the sanction of exclusion from the society where they discerned that it was warranted. On a visit to Pelton near Newcastle upon Tyne in 1764, Wesley found that since his last visit sixty-four members of the Society had been expelled:

2 for cursing and swearing
2 for habitual Sabbath-breaking
17 for drunkenness
2 for retailing spirituous liquors
2 for quarrelling and brawling
1 for beating his wife
1 for habitual, wilful lying
1 for railing and evil-speaking
1 for idleness and laziness
29 for lightness and carelessness.

All this presupposes not only a church society, but also a village society in which everyone's behaviour was intimately known to their neighbours. It also supposes that the offensive and ungodly behaviours displayed were wilful and persistent, that friendly warnings and admonitions had been spurned or mocked. It also shows that, unlike the situation today when the church is only supposed to care about sexual misdemeanours, the early Methodists were concerned about every aspect of a godly life and example.

Drunkenness was one of the curses of the 18th century, as it is today. The Methodists understood the nature of alcoholism sufficiently to know that once a drunkard had dried out, even a drop of alcohol could revive the craving. So the whole Methodist movement embraced teetotalism as a way of sharing the burden of the alcoholic and to avoid offence for 'the weaker brethren.'

In accordance with the Apostle's instruction, the Methodists accepted that, 'It is better not to eat meat or to drink wine or to do anything else that will cause your brother to fall' (Rom 14.21). Methodist abstinence is a noble example of the spirit of loving concern that led some to renounce an allowable pleasure for the sake of others who found it hard to avoid excess.

It is easy to see that, exercised in the wrong spirit, the Methodist system of pastoral care and discipline in band and class could become inquisitorial and oppressive. But exercised in a spirit of love for one another, as it was, the system underpinned the evangelical revivals of the 18th and 19th centuries, that brought many men and women to a strong and mature Christian faith, and which, through the influence of such men and women, changed the face of the nation.

Today, we might prefer a less formal or structured approach than Wesley's, but we cannot avoid the need to watch over one another if we are truly to love one another in Christ. When people become Christians or begin to enquire about our faith, they are coming out of a world and a culture whose standards and values are far from godly. Their personal, sexual and family relationships may be chaotic. Their business and financial practices may be unethical or even unlawful. They may be in the habit of lying, cheating and stealing. They may be addicted to drink, drugs, pornography or gambling.

It is absurd to suppose that they are going to be able to reorder their lives either overnight or by themselves. They will need a place where they can be open; they need a person or a group of people who will support and encourage them, and hold them to account, and who will tell them bluntly, if need be, 'You can't do that.'

The whole process will take time, in the end a lifetime. But the outline of a godly life needs to be put in place sooner rather than later, if it is to be put in place at all.

Experience with many people going through the Alpha course, is that often the Holy Spirit will convict a person as they draw nearer to God of the things in their lives that need to be changed. For example, Vicky was living with her little girl and her partner Ian when a friend suggested that she start coming to church. Vicky had had no previous experience of this or any other church and was only conscious of something missing in her life.

Another friend then leant her the Alpha book *Questions of Life.* Reading this, Vicky found what was missing and asked Jesus to come into her life and be her Lord and Saviour. She knew then that she needed to put her relationship with Ian on a more godly footing.

While she was attending the Alpha Course itself she talked to Ian about getting married sooner rather than later. Coming to church with Vicky and seeing the changes in her, Ian also became open to God. They were married some months later, and Ian attended the next Alpha Course and became a Christian too.

But the refashioning of a person's life after conversion is not always so painless, nor can we assume that a committed Christian will never fall again into grave and serious sin.

Then, church discipline is only the outworking of love – tough love - for the sinner. The Letter to the Hebrews says, 'No discipline seems pleasant at the time, but painful. Later on, however, it produces a fruit of righteousness and peace for those who have been trained by it.' (Hebrews 12.11).

Every parent knows that they do their children no favours by letting them do as they please all the time. God is a good parent, and sometimes he uses the church as his instrument of discipline.

The church is indeed a come-as-you-are party, but it is not a stay-as-you-are party. As Paul expounds the doctrine of justification by faith in the letter to the Romans, he comes to the point where he asks twice over, 'What shall we say then? Shall we go on sinning, so that grace may increase? … What then? Shall we sin because we are not under law but under grace?' (Romans 6.1, 15).

To each question he replies, 'By no means!' To ask the question is to reveal an incomprehension both of the nature of sin and of the nature of redemption. We have been saved so that we can stop sinning and live that life of freedom and happiness for which God created us.

Why would you want to sin, if you did not have to?

Jesus told a parable about a party (Luke 14.16-24 and Matthew 22.1-10). In this story a man sends out invitations to his friends, but perversely they refuse to come to the party; they all discover that they have something better to do. So the servants are sent out again to invite anyone they meet on the streets. The poor, the crippled, the lame, the blind, and the passers-by respond to the invitation with alacrity: for them, free food can't be bad.

It is an open invitation to all and sundry, 'Come as you are.' And they come. But in the version told by Matthew there is a curious postscript (Matthew 22.11-14). When the host comes in to greet his guests, one stands out from the others because he is not wearing a wedding garment. In view of the way in which they all came to the party in the first place, it might seem strange that any of them was wearing wedding clothes. But there was a custom in the Middle East that when a rich man gave such a party as this, he gave each of his guests a festal garment as they arrived.

The fault of this individual was not that he had come as he was, but that he had insisted on staying as he was.

Paul exhorts us, 'as God's chosen people, holy and beloved, clothe yourselves with compassion, kindness, humility, gentleness and patience. Bear with each other and forgive whatever grievances you may have against one another. Forgive as the Lord forgave you. And over all these virtues put on love, which binds them all together in perfect unity' (Colossians 3.12-14).

These are the festal garments that Christ gives his guests. These are the attitudes that we have to maintain towards one another in the fellowship of his church, above all love. But it is a love that does not shrink from confrontation when a fellow guest is behaving in a way that will spoil the party, for themselves, for the other guests, or for the host.

The fate of the man in the parable was to be tied hand and foot and thrown out into the darkness. Is this a story of inclusivity, or exclusivity? It is both.

Chapter Ten

THE DANGERS OF FELLOWSHIP

It may seem strange to suggest that there can be any danger in loving each other. But anything can be corrupted, even love for one another, and we should be aware of the dangers of such corruption in order to guard against them.

The most obvious danger is that a loving fellowship becomes a 'holy huddle.' This can happen without our being aware of it. We do indeed love our fellow believers in our church or our home group; we are comfortable with them; we depend on their support and friendship; they are our family. We can easily lose the sense that, as William Temple said, 'the church is the only society on earth that exists for the benefit of non-members.'

The immediate danger of a loving fellowship is that it ceases to be outward looking. We can even arrive at a place where, without actually saying so, we do not want new people to join us. Every new person who joins the church is a new problem for the church. We may feel that we have enough problems already and would rather not take on any more. We may feel that we have adjusted to the problems of living with the people we know, and that we do not want to start all over again with people we don't know.

It may just be that we are very happy as we are, and we feel threatened by anything that would upset the status quo. This happens in small churches, especially ones where the membership is static from year to year. It also happens in smaller groups in larger churches. Pastoralia, caring for one another, is splendid, but not if it comes at the expense of mission and outreach to the lost.

There is a real tension between these two poles of church life: the pastoral and the evangelistic. If we focus our efforts and attention on reaching unbelievers, we may neglect the needs of believers. Believers need to be taught, healed, supported and nurtured, as they grow into maturity as Christians and as they encounter the obstacles and set-backs that life and the enemy inevitably put in our way.

Every church needs a well-developed and comprehensive programme for the pastoral care of its members, and for their continued growth in their knowledge and understanding of the faith and of the way in which God has meant us to live. Any church that neglects these functions will soon find that those who have just come in through the front door are going out again through the back door.

If they have to listen over and over again to the same elementary teachings about Christ and are never led on to maturity (Hebrews 6.1), or if their own needs for strength and comfort and healing in the face of attacks from the world, the flesh, and devil go unmet, then they will either fall away from God altogether or will find another church that more fully meets their needs.

On the other hand, there are churches that are so focussed on the ministries of healing, physical, emotional and spiritual, on teaching ever more obscure points of doctrine, or on guarding their members against ever more subtle temptations, that they never have time to make new disciples: they are too busy discipling the one's they have got.

This is a challenge for church leaders: to build into the structures of the church the programmes and activities that address both these two challenges. But it is also a challenge for every church member: to hold in balance their own needs with the needs of others, especially those outside the church who are separated from Christ, without hope and without God in the world.

Every group in the church, whether it is the congregation as a whole, or smaller sub-groups such as house fellowships or pastorates, needs to have in mind both the needs of its own members and the needs of those at present outside the circle.

This is one of the secrets of a healthy and growing church: to be a community of people that love one another, but also a community that is always open to new people joining it. A fire will die down, and eventually go out, unless it is constantly fed with fuel. The fuel that keeps a church on fire is a constant supply of new Christians.

The activities and programmes that produce this fuel, must then be complemented by other activities and programmes that nurture, teach and support these new Christians through every stage of their earthly lives, and on into the life of the world to come.

The second danger of loving one another lies in the transgression of the sexual boundaries. These are temptations that are with us in every walk of life. They can be especially strong in a charismatic church.

The old, Anglo-Saxon, aversion to physical contact with one another has now broken down everywhere: footballers embrace and kiss one another when they score a goal; we have all become more tactile in our daily lives. But this happened in the Christian fellowship before it happened on the football field or in the world at large. One of the early fruits and signs of the charismatic renewal was that Spirit-filled Christians rediscovered the instruction to 'greet one another with a holy kiss' (1 Corinthians 16.20). But when does a holy kiss become an unholy kiss?

No one is immune to sexual temptation, and everyone has transgressed in one way or another. When the Pharisees brought to Jesus a woman taken in adultery, they challenged Jesus to condemn her (John 8.2-11). Jesus refused. At first he bent down and wrote with his finger on the ground. Scripture does not tell us what he wrote or even if what he wrote was of any significance in the case.

The most amusing guess that I have heard is that Jesus began to write in the dust the names of the women about whom the men around him had entertained lustful fantasies, if not more – Rachel, Miriam, Hannah ... Certain it is, that as Jesus challenged anyone without sin in his life to throw the first stone, they all began to go away, starting with the eldest.

This should be a warning to us, not only against throwing stones at other sinners, but also against thinking that anyone is safe from sexual temptations. They inevitably arise in the church, in the home group, and in every other context in which we come into close proximity with other people.

From puberty onwards, life is a constant exercise in controlling our sexual impulses and keeping them within the boundaries that God has prescribed for our own good. For some people this is easier than for others, but who knows when temptation will arise for any of us, and sometimes it can come with terrifying power.

It is as well for the church, and for us as individuals, to put in place safeguards to protect and strengthen each other against such temptations. One of the joys of life together in the church is that we are surrounded by people of all ages, newborn babies, children growing up from infancy, teenagers, young adults courting, marrying, having families, people in the prime of life, people growing old, retiring, slowing down, becoming frail and eventually going to be with the Lord forever.

The church is indeed the Lord's family and it is an enormous privilege to belong to such a local congregation as this. So many older people in the world today are deprived of the company of children and young people; so many children and young parents are deprived of the support of the older generation; so many parents are bringing up children on their own; so many children are deprived of either a father or a mother figure.

The church is a family of all ages, redeeming us from the effects of the disintegration of community and family life that is a trait of our modern society. But just as natural families are not immune from sexual follies, such as incest and child abuse, neither is the Lord's family.

There are, or should be, taboos in place to restrain us, but sometimes these taboos are broken. There have been only too many well-publicised cases of child abuse within the church, or of vicars having affairs with the organist or the church secretary, for us to be complacent about our relationships as Christians.

Most churches today have a Child Protection Policy to protect, not only the church's children from abuse, but also the adults from temptation. According to such policies, an adult should not normally be alone with a child, either in a room or in a car. Special care is taken in children's groups about supervising children's visits to the toilet. Touching, cuddling, and picking up children, even in public, is discouraged, except where a child is hurt or upset.

Such rules may seem petty and unnecessary, but the days of our innocence with regard to the relationships of adults and children are over, and churches need to have sensible safeguards in place.

When it comes to relationships between adults, we all have to police ourselves, keeping watch over our words and actions. Billy Graham had a life-long rule never to be alone in a car with a woman, except his wife. Perhaps as a result of this rule, there was never a hint of scandal during Billy Graham's long career; not for him the spectacular fall from grace that has overtaken other high-profile evangelists and ministers.

As a strict rule for everyday life it might not work, but it is a good warning: the enclosed privacy of a car invites intimacy, and we do well to beware of putting ourselves in compromising situations. It is not only inappropriate touching that can lead to sin, but inappropriate conversation, in the car or anywhere else.

We are of course most at risk of temptation if our own marriages are not happy and satisfying. But it is never appropriate to discuss the state of your marriage or your sex life with another person of the opposite sex. If these subjects need to be discussed, then they should be discussed with someone of the same sex, and preferably with someone appointed and trained by the church to deal with these areas of Christian life.

It is not only serious conversations that can be inappropriate; Paul tells us, 'Do not let any unwholesome talk come out of your mouths … Nor should there be obscenity, foolish talk or coarse joking, which are out of place' (Ephesians

4.29 and 5.4). Paul was only too aware of the possibility of sexual immorality within the church, and these warnings are in the context of forestalling even the beginnings of such behaviour.

There are similar Scriptural warnings about dress: Paul says, 'I also want women to dress modestly, with decency and propriety,' (1 Timothy 2.9). Jesus warns men that to look lustfully at a woman is the same sin as adultery, (Matthew 5.28). The equivalent sin in a woman is to dress in such a way as to encourage men to look lustfully at her.

A generation ago the stereotype of the evangelical Christian girl was of one dressed in a fawn twin-set and flat, sensible shoes. There is no Scriptural prohibition against style, colour or even chic. Modesty, decency and propriety are something else. They are for the most part culturally defined, but we all know where the boundaries are in our own society, and both men and women are to observe them, not for the sake of dowdiness but for the sake of not leading each other into temptation.

Most churches have rules about prayer and counselling that forbid a man ministering to a woman, or a woman to a man, at least on their own, whatever their need. We rightly pray for one another, after the example of Scripture, with the laying on of hands. But we have to be sensitive and careful about where and how we lay hands on one another.

All these considerations can be met with a certain impatience in the church: 'as if we would do that sort of thing.' But it is naïve to suppose that any of us would not do 'that sort of thing' in the wrong circumstances and under the wrong sort of provocation. Part of loving one another, is not to put ourselves or one another in situations where we might be tempted beyond what we can bear. God does not do it (1 Corinthians 10.13), so neither should we.

A third corruption of the blessing of mutual love is manifest in the cults. The Moonies make a salutary case study. The Moonies is the popular name for the so-called 'Unification Church' founded in 1954 in South Korea by Sun Myung Moon.

Since 1954, the Moonies have spread throughout the world, being particularly strong in the United States and South America. In the 1970s and 1980s the Moonies attracted much adverse publicity on account of their methods of recruitment. A classic story from the inside was *Escape from the Moonies* by Susan and Anne Swatland (New English Library 1982).

More recently suspicion of the Moonies, and of Moon in particular, have centred on their political influence in the USA, but there is no reason to suppose that their recruitment methods have changed. Many others have come forward and told similar stories to that of Susan Swatland, down to the present day.

There are five features of the programme by which young people in particular are trapped into membership of the Moonies:

- 'Heavenly Deception', by which potential recruits are misled about the nature of the invitation to which they are responding and of the group which they are joining.
- 'Love Bombing', by which potential recruits are surrounded by expressions of love and concern, often expressed by caring touch.
- Deprivation of privacy, by which recruits are constantly in the company of other cult

members who intrude into their activities and their thoughts, day and night.

- Deprivation of sleep, by which initiates are allowed only a few hours of sleep each night, making them susceptible to thought control and suggestion.
- Deprivation of former and family contacts, by which members are cut off from any others who might question or reject the teachings of the leaders of the cult.

It is useful to look at the life of the Christian fellowship in contrast to the methods of the Moonies. First, we serve Jesus who is the Truth. There is no place for any sort of deception in our approach to non-believers.

If we are inviting friends to an Alpha Course, we must make it clear that this is not only 'a chance to explore the meaning of life,' but also a simple explanation of the Christian faith. If we are inviting neighbours to a coffee morning or business colleagues to a dinner at which a Christian will give their testimony, we must make it clear that this is not only a coffee morning or a dinner party, but an opportunity to hear someone's story as a Christian.

We should not 'bomb' people with love. Love is something that grows slowly and naturally between people, even in a supernatural context. There is a proper reticence and reserve about love in the early stages of an acquaintance or friendship. Those who welcome people at the church door need to be sensitive about whom to hug and kiss, and whose hand to shake. We all have a sense of personal space around us, and few of us want that personal space invaded except by mutual invitation.

Love is not a form of manipulation. True love always means giving another person the time and space to make free choices, uninfluenced by our wishes, even our best wishes, for them.

In a world in which many people are deprived of love, feeling lost and lonely, the embrace of a loving fellowship can be an extremely attractive proposition – and indeed I have been arguing in this book that the love that we have to offer in the church is an important aspect of the Gospel. Yet, we have to be careful that our love is not offered on condition of people accepting our beliefs and joining our fellowship.

There are opponents of the Gospel who accuse us of this very thing, and who wilfully refuse to see the difference between the church and the cults. We should therefore be vigilant to make sure that our love allows outsiders to approach and join the church at their own speed and of their own volition, or not to join at all as the case may be.

This can be frustrating, when we are sure that the faith and the life that we have to offer is the best for everyone. But from the beginning of Creation, God has given his human creatures the space and the right to choose, to choose to obey or disobey, to believe or disbelieve. What God has given, we have no right to take away.

We can sometimes feel that our Christian discipleship keeps us busy, morning, noon and night. By the time we have served God in our families, through our work, in our leisure activities and in the church, we have little enough time to relax. Indeed we can become stressed and tired by the commitments we undertake.

On the one hand, this is as it should be: servants should expect to be tired at the end of the day. On the other hand, God has a plan for us to rest, as well as to serve.

The original intention of the Sabbath was rest, and however we interpret that in our lives as Christians, we need to preserve the principle and intention of the Sabbath, and rest from our labours. What we allow and value for ourselves, we must also allow and value for others, non-believers as well as believers.

Christians positively need time on their own with God, time to reflect, time to pray, time to seek both the guidance and the peace that God gives. People approaching the Christian faith need similar time and space.

Finally, it is not part of belonging to the Christian fellowship that we lose touch with former contacts, with family and friends, whether they are also Christians or not. Indeed, it is a positive responsibility for Christians to try to keep up those contacts, for how else will the outside world hear the good news of the love of God.

Christian beliefs and the Christian life do not need to be protected from questioning and dispute. We can enter into the market-place or the battle-field of ideas, confident that we have the truth and confident that '*magna est veritas et praevalebit'*: 'great is the truth and it will prevail'.

The market-place and the battle-field are not the most comfortable places to be. There is a constant temptation for Christians to retreat into the safety of the company of 'like-minded people.' But it is a temptation that we have to resist. Our place is as much out there in the world that Jesus came to save, as it is in the fellowship of the saved. The lifeboat must go out again and again to search for those in peril on the sea; as long as it sits in the lifeboat station it is not a lifeboat at all.

But we should not be overcome by fear of the dangers of fellowship. The church in most places is not in any immediate danger of falling into the traps that we have examined above. For the most part we are not in danger of becoming a cult. Despite the high-profile scandals of sexual impropriety in the press, most churches are remarkably free, considering the world we live in, from sexual indiscretions, and most churches are too frightened of extinction to behave like a complacent, holy huddle.

So, although we should be aware of the dangers of loving each other, we should not be at all deterred from doing it. Our generation is more in danger of a paralysis of fear, fears about all the perils that surround us. In spite of the fact that we live longer, more secure lives than ever before, we are obsessed by the fear of epidemics, of the abduction of our children, of accidents, of crime. Health and Safety legislation has become absurd, and the fear of litigation makes everyone afraid of exposing others to even normal hazards.

Christians should not buy into this culture of fear, but boldly and freely enter into the inheritance that we have in Jesus, part of which is to enjoy the love and companionship of our fellow human beings of all ages in the fellowship of the church.

Chapter Eleven

FELLOWSHIP AND SOLITUDE

The fellowship of other Christians is not a substitute for a personal relationship with God. Indeed the fellowship of the church can only work properly if it is the fellowship of a group of people who each have their own personal relationship with God, and this relationship can only be formed and cultivated in solitude.

Whatever time we spend with friends in the Lord must be balanced by time that we spend with God on our own. Some may call it their Quiet Time, others their Prayer Time, but without it our relationship with God quickly becomes second-hand and unreal.

When Jesus was teaching his disciples to pray he said, 'Go into your room, close the door and pray to your Father, who is unseen. Then your Father, who sees what is done in secret, will reward you,' (Matthew 6.6).

Jesus tells us to seek out times and places of solitude and silence. It is not a law that this has to be in our own rooms. People who have to share their living space with others, may find that difficult. There are other places where silence and personal space can be found: the open air, quiet churches, even a shared house or apartment in the dead of night.

Susannah, the mother of John and Charles Wesley, used to sit down in her rocking chair in the kitchen, surrounded by her numerous progeny, and put her apron over her face, and her numerous progeny knew to leave her alone while the apron remained in place – their mother was praying. The essentials are that we do not have to speak or respond to anyone else during this time.

Many people in our society find solitude and silence oppressive. They avoid it if they possibly can, and in this technological age that is only too easy. Every minute of the day and night can be filled with sound, and with interaction with other people.

In many households the radio or the television are switched on the moment someone wakes, indeed some people are woken up by the radio automatically coming on with the alarm clock.

The mobile phone is an ever present companion, claiming our attention in the house, in the car, in the train, at the office, in the playground, walking along the street. We need never be out of touch with our friends and family, talking or texting. At work an email comes pinging in on our computers and we click over to see who it is and what it says.

The 21st century equivalent of 'go into your room and close the door,' means also take out the ear-plugs of your iPod, switch off your mobile phone and leave it outside the room, turn off the computer, the radio and the television, and tell everyone around you, like Susannah Wesley, that you do not wish to be disturbed.

We have serious business to do with God and it is business that can only be done in solitude and silence. In the end it is business that does not concern anyone else but me. It concerns the most inward secrets of my heart, secrets to which I alone, and the God who sees and knows everything, have access. It concerns the most important matters in my life, my past, my present and my future.

Counselling, or talking things through with Christian friends, can help us to face up to the guilt and traumas of the past, but in the end the only place that they can be resolved is on our own with God. The advice and experience of others can help us to sort out the issues that we face in our lives today, and help us to make up our minds about the dilemmas we face about the future. But in the end, the only place where we can find the peace that we seek is in the secret place with God.

As we look at the people in the Bible we see that many of the most important turning points in the lives of these godly men and women took place at times when they were alone with God. It has to be said that many of these experiences were, and are, not easy or pleasant ones.

Perhaps that is why so many people try to escape such times of solitude and silence. It can seem so much easier to drift, or be carried along by the crowd and the demands of everyday life, to distract or anaesthetise ourselves, with drink or drugs, with work or sex, or the company of friends, to live in the present moment and to avoid the call of God. But the promise of Jesus is that those who will do as he says, who will seek out the times and places of solitude and silence with the heavenly Father, will find a reward.

It was in the silence of the night that the boy Samuel first heard the voice of God. (1 Samuel 3.1-10).

Hushed was the evening hymn,
The temple courts were dark;
The lamp was burning dim
Before the sacred ark;
When suddenly a voice divine
Rang through the silence of the shrine.
(James D. Burns)

Samuel was called to be a prophet, to listen to the voice of God and tell God's people what the Lord had said. Moses longed for the day when all the Lord's people would be prophets, in the sense that they could all hear the voice of God for themselves and not need someone else to tell them what the Lord was saying.

Jeremiah prophesied that such a day was coming when, 'No longer will a man teach his neighbour, or a man his brother, saying, "Know the Lord," because they will all know me from the least of them to the greatest, declares the Lord,' (Jeremiah 31.34).

This prophecy was fulfilled on the Day of Pentecost when the Holy Spirit came. He enables us all, young and old, to hear the voice of God as he speaks to us about himself and about our lives and about our relationship to him.

As we 'go into our rooms and close the door' our first words to God should be those of the child Samuel, 'Speak, Lord, your servant is listening.' Or as it says in the Psalms, 'I will listen to what God the Lord will say,' (Psalm 85.8).

The best and surest way to hear what the Lord says is through the Scriptures. The Scriptures are a record of what God has said in the past, and God does not change his mind or his word. 'God spoke to our forefathers through the prophets in many and various ways, and in these last days he has spoken to us by his Son,' (Hebrews 1.1-2).

What God spoke through the prophets and what God revealed of himself through his Son was written down for us, to be an everlasting witness for the days to come. The first place we must turn when we seek God in the secret place is to his Word in Scripture.

For Christians, meditation or contemplation does not consist of emptying the mind, as it does in many Eastern religions, but it consists of filling the mind with the Word of God. However we choose to do this, by reading steadily through the books of the Bible, by using a church lectionary, or by following the guidance of commentaries or notes, we can rely on God to speak to us out of his Word. But a quiet attentiveness to the voice of God is necessary if we are to hear from him.

Elijah was saved from a time of despair and depression by hearing the voice of God. He had seen the power of God displayed on Mount Carmel. The prophets of Baal had been put to shame, and God had vindicated his own Name before the king and all the people of Israel. The Lord had sent fire and rain in accordance with the prayer of his servant Elijah (1 Kings 17-18). But Queen Jezebel threatened his life, and Elijah fled in terror.

Elijah's spirit failed him and, sitting under a broom tree, he uttered the immortal words, 'I've had enough.' Here is one of the two towering figures of the Old Testament, Moses and Elijah, standing for the Law and the Prophets, the God-given guides of his people Israel, and he has had enough.

We need not beat ourselves up too much if we sometimes find ourselves in the place where we feel like sitting down and saying, 'I've had enough.' One of the greatest of the men of God had reached the same place in his life. But by the grace of God he went on. He made his way to the mountain of God, Horeb or Sinai, where Moses before him had met with God and heard from God. At Horeb, Elijah had a profound experience of the mercy and patience of God.

First, God caused Elijah to see again manifestations of his power and glory. In one of the most dramatic stories in the Bible,

> *A great and powerful wind tore the mountains apart and shattered the rocks before the Lord. But the Lord was not in the wind. After the wind there was an earthquake. But the Lord was not in the earthquake. After the earthquake came a fire. But the Lord was not in the fire. And after the fire came a gentle whisper.* (1 Kings 19.11-12)

Translators have differed over how to render this last expression. In the King James Version it is rendered, 'a still, small voice.' But it was in that still, small voice that onward came the Lord. The Lord spoke to Elijah in the stillness, 'What are you doing here, Elijah?' and he told Elijah what to do.

The best place to go in our own times of depression or despair, or when we are afraid of what the future may hold, is that secret place where we meet with God the Father. We may not have the same dramatic encounter with God that Elijah had, but we can expect to return, strengthened and guided, as Elijah was, about the way forward.

Such times with God, if they do nothing else, restore to us a sense of perspective and hope. Even our worst troubles and afflictions are, as Paul says, light and momentary, compared with the eternal glory that will far outweigh them all (2 Corinthians 4.17). We do not face any of life's trials and tribulations alone, but surrounded and supported by the everlasting arms of God, a loving heavenly Father who cares for us and encourages us to cast all our cares on him.

Jacob had a different sort of wrestling to do with God when he found himself alone, on his way home from the house of Laban. Jacob had left his father Isaac's house under a cloud. He had deceived and alienated his brother Esau by depriving him by trickery, first of his birth-right and then of his blessing.

Like Elijah he fled in fear of his life. But in the country of his uncle Laban, Jacob made his fortune, found, not one, but two wives, and fathered twelve children by them and their maids. Eventually, God told him to return to face his brother Esau. At the brook Jabbok, he sent on ahead of him his wives and children and all his flocks and herds, and gifts to propitiate Esau before he met him. Then we read, 'Jacob was left alone,' (Genesis 32.24).

All that night Jacob wrestled with God. It is clear enough why Jacob needed to wrestle, not only with the angel of God, but also with himself. At last he had to face up to the sort of person he had been: a trickster and deceiver. It is not only his brother Esau that he had to confront but his own conscience in the sight of God.

This is why being left alone with God can be an unsettling and uncomfortable experience: we have to face up to the sort of people that we are and the sort of things that we have done. It may be that only God knows about some of those things, but God knows and we have to account for them to him. Reaching the place where we know ourselves to be reconciled with God and assured of his blessing is not necessarily a quick and easy process. It took Jacob all night until the sun rose.

In the accounts of the classic revivals in history, sinners who come under conviction of sin often wrestle with God in prayer for hours before they come through to a place of peace and joy as they find assurance of salvation through the blood of Jesus. There is indeed no other way to find salvation, but the time is taken in bringing ourselves to face and accept our own sinfulness without excuse and without prevarication, in taking responsibility for ourselves and our actions without recrimination or putting the blame on others. 'It's me, it's me, it's me, O Lord, standing in the need of prayer.'

Jacob changed that night. The change is symbolised in the change of name, from Jacob to Israel. We shall be changed when we have the courage to be left alone with God and to wrestle with him over our sins and failures. But we too will find Jacob's blessing, because God is ever merciful, and does not keep his anger forever.

Jacob then has to face his brother Esau and to make peace with him. But this proved surprisingly easy after his experience at Peniel, and when they met Esau's face was as the face of God.

Like Jacob, we also have to go out from the place of wrestling with God to face those in the world whom we have injured and offended and to make our peace with them as best we can. But it is always easier, when we have already made our peace with God.

Above all, of course, our example of seeking God in the place of solitude is Jesus. Immediately after his baptism in the river Jordan, Jesus was led out by the Holy Spirit into the wilderness (Matthew 4.1). Since this was the impulse of the Holy Spirit this long period of silence and solitude must have been a necessity for Jesus. If such times of solitude and silence were necessary for Jesus, how much more so for us!

Only those who have been physically in the desert can understand the complete and utter silence that surrounded Jesus in those forty days. There is no silence like the silence of the desert: no bird, no animal, no vegetation rustling in the breeze, no human voice, no engine, no sound. There, Jesus faced the temptations associated with his knowledge of who he was and of the mission and task for which God had prepared him.

The place of solitude and silence is the place where we too can face our own temptations. In some measure all of us who are in Christ share Christ's temptations: to put our own comforts and satisfactions before the call of God; to use stunts or to take short cuts to court publicity or to curry favour with the world. But we also face the temptations that are common to mankind, the temptations of the world and the flesh, as well as the devil.

When we first become Christians we have to re-examine all our aims and ambitions, our visions and values. It takes some time, even a lifetime. The Holy Spirit will question all sorts of habits and traits that we have taken for granted in the way that we live our lives, habits that we may not even have been aware of, and traits that we may even have been proud of. But the process of facing and overcoming our temptations does not stop after forty days, either for Jesus or for us.

We find Jesus retiring into lonely places again and again in order to pray and come before his heavenly Father with major decisions that he had to take, and no doubt the occasions that are mentioned in Scripture are but a few notable incidents in a life in which engagement with the world was always balanced by withdrawal.

Soon after the beginning of his ministry in Galilee, the people of Capernaum wanted to hold on to Jesus, to keep him amongst them as their own personal healer and teacher, and so successful had his ministry been that no doubt this was also a temptation for Jesus. So, 'very early in the morning, while it was still dark, Jesus got up, left the house and went off to a solitary place, where he prayed' (Mark 1.35).

This time spent on his own with God must have cleared his mind because, coming back into town, he announced that he would move on to the other villages, because he was called to preach the gospel to them also.

Before choosing and nominating twelve of his disciples to be Apostles, Jesus spent the night praying to God (Luke 6.12). He had previously called a number of men to be his followers, and there was a larger company of people, both men and women, who accompanied him as he travelled from place to place, heard what he said, and saw what he did.

Out of this assorted group he needed to choose twelve to extend the work of the Kingdom and to be the foundation stones of the church that he would build. It was, and is, always important to choose the right people for the job, whatever that job may be. Jesus chose in prayer.

Luke tells us that 'Jesus often withdrew to lonely places and prayed' (Luke 5.16). So it is no surprise to find that at the most decisive moment in his life he also sought out silence and solitude in the Garden of Gethsemane. He did not spend those last few hours of his life drawing strength from the company of his friends and followers, much as he needed the sense of their support.

Even less did he spend those hours in some sort of distraction, but he chose to spend them alone with his heavenly Father in prayer. He must face his fears and his natural shrinking from pain and death. He must make sure that this is the only way for him to fulfil his calling. He must confront who-knows-what demons and their insidious voices.

This is the only place where he can prepare himself for what lies ahead and find that inner peace that will enable him to go through his ordeal with a calm control, not only of himself, but of events as they unfold.

It is the cultivation of this habit of finding God in the secret place that will enable us to cope with whatever challenges we encounter, in life and in facing death. It will enable us to respond better when these challenges come upon us unawares and we have to make an immediate response.

Such times are an indispensable complement to the times that we spend in corporate praise and worship, and the times that we spend in the company and fellowship of other Christians.

As well as the habit of such daily times of withdrawal, there is also room in our Christian lives for more extended periods of silence. When I was first ordained as a curate, our rector used to put all the church's pastoral staff in the car in the first week in December and take us off to the Community of the Resurrection, an Anglican monastery in Yorkshire. There we spent the week in silence, joining in the regular worship of the monks, led in a series of devotional addresses by one of the brethren of the Community, but otherwise left to communicate with God in silence. I remember the sense of relief as the silence descended upon us after Compline on the first evening, knowing that I would not have to talk to anyone for the next four days. It was like a warm, fleecy, blanket in which I could wrap myself up.

I loved those times alone with God. They were not always times of inward tranquillity or peace, but they were always times of refreshment, and a recovery of direction and vision. I kept up the practice of an annual retreat throughout the years of my ministry.

Not far away from wherever you live there is a similar religious community of monks or nuns, which offers the opportunity to come away and spend a few days or even a few weeks with God. It is possible to make a private retreat or to join a group, to seek spiritual guidance from a member of the community, or to be entirely self-directed. It is helpful to spend such time in the presence of others who are used to silence and have made silence their way of life.

Gerard Manley Hopkins was a Catholic priest who chose such a life with the Society of Jesus, and who wrote about 'elected silence':

Elected Silence, sing to me
And beat upon my whorlèd ear,
Pipe me to pastures still, and be
The music that I care to hear.

Another Christian poet, T. S. Eliot, also wrote about the experience of silence:

I said to my soul, be still,
and let the dark come upon you
Which shall be the darkness of God.

In case anyone should doubt that it is appropriate to speak of the darkness of God, there is in Scripture a 'thick darkness' that has nothing to do with the Enemy, but is the place where God dwells (Exodus 20.21). It is the 'cloud of unknowing' where the God who passes all understanding makes himself known.

It is only in silence that this God can be found. It is in this place that Paul was 'caught up into the third heaven … and heard inexpressible things that man cannot tell' (2 Corinthians 12.2-4). Who can say whether such an experience will not be granted to others who seek God in solitude. One way or another, 'your Father, who sees what is done in secret, will reward you.'

Chapter Twelve

THE SECRET OF FELLOWSHIP

The secret of Christian fellowship is to keep looking up and to keep looking out.

The source of Christian unity is God, who is One. When Paul is urging the Christians in Ephesus to keep the unity of the Spirit, he bases his call on the Oneness of God:

> *There is one body and one Spirit – just as you were called to one hope when you were called – one Lord, one faith, one baptism; one God and Father of us all, who is over all and through all and in all.* (Ephesians 4.4-6)

Since God is One, Christians find their oneness in this One God. But even here there is confusion in the world today. God is One, but that is not the same thing as saying that there is only one god. There are plainly many gods in the world today, just as there were in days of old. As well as their own God, Yahweh, the God of Abraham, Isaac and Jacob, the Jews knew that there were other gods, the gods of the nations round about: the Canaanite Baals, Chemosh the god of the Moabites, and Molech the god of the Ammonites.

The Hindus still worship many gods. The New Testament also suggests that there are many secular, material things that become gods in our lives, like money and the belly. Even within the monotheistic religions of the world, it is not true to say that, because they all believe in one god, therefore they all believe in the same god: Christians, Jews, and Moslems all nominally worship the same God, the God of Abraham, Isaac and Jacob. But faced with the unbelief and malice of some of the Jews, Jesus told them that in practice their true father was the devil, (John 8.44). Strong words, but not mine.

Likewise, the god who spoke to Mohammed denied that he had a son, while the Christian God says, 'This is my beloved Son.' Clearly they cannot be the same god. Only those who know nothing of any religion think that all religions are the same and worship the same god. We, Christians, find our oneness in worshipping the One God and Father of our Lord Jesus Christ.

Any group of people is held together either by some common experience or some common interest. It might be a reunion of war veterans or a passion for playing golf. The Christian fellowship is held together first and foremost by an experience of the grace of God mediated to them through the person of Jesus Christ.

There is no blue-print for this experience; it is as varied as the needs and longings of the human heart. But in one way or another Christians have in common an experience of the presence, the power, and the love of God, mediated to them through Jesus.

We do not necessarily have anything else in common. As we have seen, from the beginning the church has been made up of people of different social classes, different nationalities and languages, different races and cultures, of both sexes and of all ages. Therefore it is imperative that we keep our eyes on the One to whom we owe our life and our salvation: God, the Father, the Son and the Holy Spirit.

In practice, this means that worship and prayer are the core activities of the Christian fellowship. It is through these that we are reminded of what God has done for us, in creation and redemption; our hearts and minds are lifted up above our immediate and often petty preoccupations to sit with Christ in the heavenly places, to join in song with the angels, and to share a foretaste of the life that is to come.

God is from everlasting to everlasting; Jesus Christ is the same, yesterday, today and forever. We may be in a place of prosperity and blessing or we may be in a place of suffering and loss. But it is still appropriate to praise God and rejoice in our hope.

In the lands of Old Christendom, we have developed a casual and complacent attitude to corporate worship. We take it for granted that we can meet together for worship whenever and wherever we want, and we tend likewise to excuse ourselves from worship whenever and wherever we want.

It is the Christians in other parts of the world who are forbidden to worship or who are persecuted for worshipping who realise the true value of corporate worship. Christians in China or in Muslim countries take extraordinary risks to meet together, to praise God, and to strengthen one another through mutual fellowship. Worshipping together is at the heart of Christian unity; it is this shared experience that binds us together in love.

Prayer is an expression of our dependence on God for all things. We may be thanking God for his blessings or laying our anxieties before him: either way, we are expressing the fact that every good and perfect gift comes from him, and that we are as dependent on his mercy and provision as a new-born child is dependent on its mother's milk.

If your church publishes a membership roll, it is a good discipline to pray through the roll, lifting one another up to God for his grace and mercy. When we meet together in smaller groups there should be a time for sharing both our joys and sorrows, and for praying for each other's needs. Praying for each other and praying together are expressions of our solidarity with one another in the Body of Christ. We stand together in our mutual dependence on God, seeking his provision, not only for our own needs, but also for one another's.

The best way to overcome the irritation or anger that we sometimes feel towards other members of the church is to pray for them. Jesus taught us by word and example to love our enemies, and the way to do it is to pray for them (Matthew 5.44). This applies to those outside the church who actively oppose or persecute us, but it also applies to those inside the church whom we find it difficult to love.

When the people of Israel returned from their exile in Babylon, there was still much in their national life that displeased the Lord, but we read that 'those who feared the Lord talked to each other and the Lord listened and heard' (Malachi 3.16).

When Christians meet together and talk about the Lord, what he has done for them, and what they look to him to do for them, the Lord listens. It is said that the Holy Spirit always turns up when people talk about Jesus, just because he loves listening to people talking about Jesus.

Certainly in my experience that is true. Wherever the Lord's people talk about Jesus, whether in the church or in the home or in the street, the anointing of the Holy Spirit falls upon them, and upon anyone else who happens to be listening to them. In the company of non-believers this is often manifest in outbursts of irrational hostility, but in the company of believers, it is manifest in a sense of peace and joy.

But if our primary focus in the Christian fellowship is upon God then our secondary focus must be on the world which God loved so much that he sent his only Son, that all who believe in him should not perish but have everlasting life.

We cannot focus on Jesus without focusing on the Great Commission, to go into the world and make disciples of every nation, including our own. So, the secret of fellowship is to keep looking up, to God, and to keep looking out, to the world that is still unsaved: 'the church is the only society on earth that exists for the benefit of non-members.'

When we surveyed people's experience of fellowship in the Fountain of Life we found that one of the principle places where people had made friends was in working together in one of the church teams. It might have been the team who are responsible for coffee and catering. It might have been a team leading an Alpha course. It might have been a team going out to evangelise on the streets. When we explored the secret of the growth of Hillsong, we saw that many of their friendships are made through serving together in Volunteer Teams.

In the army, soldiers in peacetime spend a lot of time in barracks, drilling and training, and taking part in mock exercises. These are often times of boredom, and these are the times when grumbles and grievances come to the surface, grumbles about the food and the pay, niggles about the officers and NCOs, and quarrels with other members of the unit.

It is when the soldiers go into battle that they bond with one another. Instead of grumbling about the food, soldiers begin to appreciate the cooks who have struggled through to set up the field kitchen and produce some sort of a hot meal. Instead of grumbling about the sergeant's pettiness, they begin to appreciate the old soldier's craft and wisdom under fire. Above all they realise their need of one another.

It is the same in the Christian 'army'. While the focus of church life is the life of the church, we shall only too easily fall into bickering and fault-finding. It is when we feel ourselves to be engaged in a common endeavour, the endeavour of making new disciples, of making Jesus known in a hostile world, of doing the works of the Kingdom, that we bond together.

When we are engaged in the work of the Kingdom we find that we cannot do it on our own; we need the gifts that God has given to other members of the Body as well as our own. It is not for nothing that the Holy Spirit divides his gifts, both the natural and the supernatural ones, apportioning to one person one gift, to another another. We quickly learn to value one another in a new way.

Bringing even one new person through to faith in Christ and a commitment to living for him is rarely the work of just one person. Vicky, whom we met earlier with her husband Ian and daughter, came to know the Lord, through the influence and love of a variety of people in the church.

Vicky and her daughter had started to go to the Christian mother-and-toddler group run by the church. There she met Andrea, who encouraged Vicky to come to church on Sundays. At church, it was Fiona who leant Vicky *Questions of Life* and supported and encouraged her through her difficult times.

Vicky was at the same time working at the local hospital alongside Chloe, a Christian nurse, with whom she had long conversations during the night about God and about Jesus. The speakers on the Alpha course explained the basic elements of the Christian life and faith to Vicky, and her group leaders listened to her questions and encouraged her and the group together to seek the answers.

At church she had made many new friends, and it was they who made her and Ian and their little girl feel welcome and at home. It is God who orchestrates these things, bringing in each person to play their part in a process that leads to another family saying, 'We have found Jesus, and our lives will never be the same again.'

Not only can Vicky and Ian rejoice, but also Andrea, Fiona, Chloe, the Alpha team, and the whole church together, valuing one another in a new way because lost sheep have been found, and they have all been used by God in different ways to search for Vicky and her family and bring them home.

It is in the more practical works of the Kingdom that Christians from across denominational divides can discover their unity again. In different places Christians are involved in many different initiatives to serve and change the society in which they live. It may be in helping the homeless or ex-prisoners. It may be in providing the poor with the necessities of life, from a food-bank to a furniture store. It may be as Street Pastors. It may be in providing counselling to women facing an unwanted pregnancy. It is in working together in such ways as these that both members of the same church and members of different churches find fellowship with one another in the name of Jesus.

All Christians are united by their allegiance to the God and Father of our Lord Jesus Christ. This should be enough to unite us all in one church or fellowship, but we have looked above at the many things that have caused division and still cause divisions within the Body of Christ. It is lamentable, but it is a fact of life.

The fellowship of the church is part of the 'now' and the 'not-yet' of the Kingdom of God. We experience it partially in the 'now', and await its fulfilment in the 'not-yet'. The best is yet to come, in the final ingathering of the People of God in the New Jerusalem.

Meanwhile, we live with a foretaste of that fellowship in the life of the church as we know it, and in the love, imperfect as it is, that we have for each other.

The very imperfection of our unity and our love for one another here and now keeps us looking forward. This world is not our home. Like Abraham we are strangers in a foreign country; our houses may look permanent, but they are only moving tents that we pitch night by night, 'a day's march nearer home.'

The tragedy of the Jews today is that they have mistaken the nature of the land that was promised to Abraham: they are still hoping and fighting for territory in the Middle East, thinking that that is their homeland. But Abraham was looking for a better country and a more abiding city – a city with foundations whose architect and builder is God, not an earthly but a heavenly country (Hebrews 11.8-9 and 13-16).

God has prepared for us just such a city and such a country. As Christians we know that our citizenship is in heaven (Philippians 3.20), from where we await our Saviour.

When Paul wrote to the Christians in Philippi he was writing to people who lived in a Roman colony. Old soldiers from the Roman army were rewarded with land and houses in colonies that became little outposts of Rome, in which people enjoyed the privileges of Roman citizenship and lived the life of Romans in a foreign land.

A century ago this was a common experience for the British, living their lives in the colonies of the British Empire, maintaining the British way of life in countries far away. We are colonists too, called to form little colonies of heaven on earth. We are not supposed to 'go native' and adopt the customs and habits of the world around us.

Rather we are to impart to the fallen world around us the beliefs and practices of a superior way of life and to invite those living in this world to abandon their former way of life and become citizens with us of a better country and a more abiding city. The life of heaven is a life of love, the love of God and the love of each other. It is a privilege and a joy to live that life, partially in this world, in all its fullness in the world to come.

* * *

Dear friends, let us love one another, for love comes from God. Everyone who loves has been born of God and knows God. Whoever does not love does not know God, because God is love. This is how God showed his love among us: He sent his one and only Son into the world that we might live through him. This is love: not that we loved God, but that he loved us and sent his Son as an atoning sacrifice for our sins. Dear friends, since God so loved us, we also ought to love one another. No one has ever seen God; but if we love one another, God lives in us and his love is made complete in us.

We know that we live in him and he in us, because he has given us of his Spirit. And we have seen and testify that the Father has sent his Son to be the Saviour of the world. If anyone acknowledges that Jesus is the Son of God, God lives in him and he in God. And so we know and rely on the love God has for us.

God is love. Whoever lives in love lives in God, and God in him. In this way, love is made complete among us so that we will have confidence on the day of judgment, because in this world we are like him. There is no fear in love. But perfect love drives out fear, because fear has to do with punishment. The one who fears is not made perfect in love.

We love because he first loved us. If anyone says, 'I love God,' yet hates his brother, he is a liar. For anyone who does not love his brother whom he has seen, cannot love God whom he has not seen. And he has given us this command: Whoever loves God must love his brother also. (1 John 4.7-21).

Lightning Source UK Ltd.
Milton Keynes UK
UKOW050224150512

192564UK00001B/2/P

9 780955 959462